The Yellow-Lighted Bookshop

The
Yellow-Lighted
Bookshop

A Memoir, a History

LEWIS BUZBEE

Graywolf Press
Saint Paul, Minnesota

Publication of this volume is made possible in part by a grant provided
by the Minnesota State Arts Board, through an appropriation by the
Minnesota State Legislature; a grant from the Wells Fargo Foundation
Minnesota; and a grant from the National Endowment for the Arts,
which believes that a great nation deserves great art. Significant support
has also been provided by the Bush Foundation; Target, with support
from the Target Foundation; the McKnight Foundation; and other gen-
erous contributions from foundations, corporations, and individuals.
To these organizations and individuals we offer our heartfelt thanks.

MINNESOTA
STATE ARTS BOARD

NATIONAL
ENDOWMENT
FOR THE ARTS

Published by Graywolf Press
2402 University Avenue, Suite 203
Saint Paul, Minnesota 55114
All rights reserved.

www.graywolfpress.org

Published in the United States of America

Excerpts from this book originally appeared in *ZYZZYVA* and
Switchback.

ISBN 1-55597-450-3

4 6 8 9 7 5 3

Library of Congress Control Number: 2005938151

Cover design: Christa Schoenbrodt, Studio Haus

Cover art: Quint Buchholz
© Sanssouci im Carl Hanser Verlag
München Wien 1997

for my mother and father

I think that I still have it in my heart someday to paint a bookshop with the front yellow and pink in the evening . . . like a light in the midst of the darkness.

Vincent van Gogh

Contents

The Yellow-Lighted Bookshop

Alone among Others

When I walk into a bookstore, any bookstore, first thing in the morning, I'm flooded with a sense of hushed excitement. I shouldn't feel this way. I've spent most of my adult life working in bookstores, either as a bookseller or a publisher's sales rep, and even though I no longer work in the business, as an incurable reader I find myself in a bookstore at least five times a week. Shouldn't I be blasé about it all by now? In the quiet of such a morning, however, the store's displays stacked squarely and its shelves tidy and promising, I know that this is no mere shop. When a bookstore opens its doors, the rest of the world enters, too, the day's weather and the day's news, the streams of customers, and of course the boxes of books and the many other worlds they contain—books of facts and truths, books newly written and those first read centuries before, books of great relevance and of absolute banality. Standing in the middle of this confluence, I can't help but feel the possibility of the universe unfolding a little, *once upon a time*.

I'm not here just to buy a new book, though. Much of

my excitement at being in a bookstore comes from the place itself, the understanding that I can stay here for as long as need be. The unspoken rules we've developed for the bookstore are quite different from the rules that govern other retail enterprises. While the bookstore is most often privately held, it honors a public claim on its time and space. It is not a big-box store where one buys closets of toilet paper or enough Tabasco sauce for the apocalypse; nor is it a tony boutique that sells prestige in the shape of sequined dresses or rare gems; and it's no convenience store either, raided for a six-pack, ciga-rettes, and a Nutty Buddy on the way home from a hard day at work. The cash register's chime does not define how long we can linger. A bookstore is for hanging out. Often for hours. Perhaps I've come to crib a recipe from a cookbook or hunt down the name of that Art Deco hotel in San Antonio or even reread one of my favorite short stories. I might browse covers awhile after meeting up with a friend, the two of us chatting about our lives. Or I can sit down in History and read the first chapter of a charming treatise on the complex language of hand gestures in high Renaissance Naples. As you might be reading right now, taking your own sweet time. If there's a café, all the better; a piece of cake and a cup of coffee, and time can run loose all over the place. I might even buy a book.

Imagine going into a department store, trying on a new jacket and walking around in it for half an hour, maybe coming back the following Wednesday to try it on again, with no real intention of buying it. Go into a pizzeria and see if you might sample a slice; you're pretty hungry, so you taste a bit of the pepperoni, the sausage, the artichoke and pineapple, and they're delicious but not quite what you're looking for that day. In other retail shops, the clerks and management are much less forgiving of those customers who would consume without paying.

Part of the allowable leisure in a bookstore comes from the product it sells. Books are slow. They require time; they are written slowly, published slowly, and read slowly. A four-hundred-page novel might take years to write, longer to publish, and even after the novel is purchased, the reader can expect to spend hours with it at one sitting over a number of days, weeks, sometimes months.

But it's not just the nature of the book that determines the bookstore's permissiveness. The modern bookstore has long been associated with the coffeehouse and the café. In eighteenth-century Europe, when coffee and tobacco conquered the continent, the coffeehouse provided a public gathering place for writers, editors, and publishers. The stimulant coffee and the sedative tobacco, in combination, made sitting at a table all day a pleasant equilibrium, perfect for writing, reading, long conversations, or staring out the window. This was the Age of Enlightenment: literacy was on the rise, books were cheaper and more abundant, and bookstores were often adjacent to coffeehouses, the customers of one were the customers of the other, with plenty of time in both for conversation and thought. Even today, the largest corporate chain stores, always mindful of the bottom line, build spaces friendly to the savor of time, with cafés and couches and study tables.

Books connect us with others, but that connection is created in solitude, one reader in one chair hearing one writer, what John Irving refers to as one genius speaking to another. It's simple to order books on-line, over the phone, or via catalogue and wait for the delivery man to scurry away before we open the door. But 90 percent of us who buy books still get out of the house and go to the bookstore, to be among the books, yes, but also to be among other book buyers, the likeminded, even if we might never say a word to them. Elias Canetti has described cafés as places we go to be "alone among others," and I've always felt this was true of the bookstore, too. It's a lovely combination, this solitude and gathering, almost as if the bookstore were the antidote for what it sold.

Perhaps the bookstore isn't as mindful of time and space as other retail shops because there isn't very much at stake. Most booksellers go into the business because they love books, and they have a natural leaning toward the mercantile life. Books are inexpensive, with a markup over wholesale that's as low as the laws of economics will traffic. Books are heavy and take up lots of space, and because each title is unique and there are so many titles a well-stocked bookstore requires, inventory and stocking create a high payroll, so most booksellers don't get paid much over minimum wage. Time may be money in the rest of the world, but not in the bookstore. There's little money here, so we can all take our time.

The bookstore has always been a marketplace where the ideas of a given period were traded, and so has played a formative role in the shaping of public discourse. The bookstore is often a stronghold in attacks against the rights of free speech. Under the aegis of Sylvia Beach's Paris store, Shakespeare and Co., *Ulysses* was first published, and without Lawrence Ferlinghetti's City Lights, Ginsberg's *Howl* might have taken years to enter the literature; these are only two of the most celebrated cases.

There is a fundamental democracy in the mass-produced book. For example, *Don Quixote*, one of the great achievements of Western literature, is roughly the same price as the most tawdry celebrity biography, maybe even a little cheaper since the nuisance of paying the author has expired. And location has little effect on the price: *Don Quixote* costs the same at the swankest New York City carriage-trade shop as in the most windswept Kansas City strip mall. Mass production in other commodities not only affects price, but also affects quality. I expect a custom-made bass guitar that costs several thousand dollars to sound and play better than my Fender knockoff, which costs two hundred. A pristine copy of the first Hogarth Press edition of Virginia Woolf's *The Waves* may be a collector's dream, but a new paperback version of it is as beguiling and compelling. The quality of her prose does not lessen with the price or edition.

In the bookstore, the finest writing is as accessible

as the most forgettable, and both are accorded the same respect: here it is, is there a reader who wants it? No matter the book, there's always someone who does. A bookstore is as likely to carry Proust's *In Search of Lost Time* as the newest book of cat cartoons, or books on automobile repair, military history, self-help, computer programming, or the evolution of microbes. There's something for everybody.

And there's somebody for everything. The bookstore is not only for the literary. Readers come with their particular obsessions to find the information they seek: the price of antique coins, effective weed eradication, the proper enclosures for small-scale pig farming. Any good bookstore carries high and low.

The book is a uniquely durable object, one that can be fully enjoyed without being damaged. A book doesn't require fuel, food, or service; it isn't very messy and rarely makes noise. A book can be read over and over, then passed on to friends, or resold at a garage sale. A book will not crash or freeze and will still work when filled with sand. Even if it falls into the bath, it can be dried out, ironed if necessary, and then finished. Should the spine of a book crack so badly the pages fall out, one simply has to gather them before the wind blows them away and wrap with a rubber band.

Most important in the democratic nature of the book, is that aside from basic literacy, books require no special training to operate.

The invitation of the bookstore occurs on so many

levels that it seems we *must* take our time. We peruse the shelves, weaving around the other customers, feeling a cold gust of rain from the open door, not really knowing what we want. Then there! on that heaped table, or hidden on the lowest, dustiest shelf, we stumble on it. A common thing, this volume. There may be five thousand copies of this particular book in the world, or fifty thousand, or half a million, all exactly alike, but this one is as rare as if it had been made solely for us. We open to the first page, and the universe unfolds, *once upon a time.*

‖‖‖‖‖

November, a dark, rainy Tuesday, late afternoon. This is my ideal time to be in a bookstore. The shortened light of the afternoon and the idleness and hush of the hour gather everything close, the shelves and the books and the few other customers who graze head-bent in the narrow aisles. There's a clerk at the counter who stares out the front window, taking a breather before the evening rush. I've come to find a book.

For the last several days I've had the sudden and general urge to buy a new book. I've stopped off at a few bookstores around the city, and while I've looked at hundreds and hundreds of books in that time, I have not found the one book that will satisfy my urge. It's not as if I don't have anything to read; there's a tower of perfectly good unread books next to my bed, not to mention the shelves of books in the living room I've been meaning to reread. I find myself, maddeningly, hungry for the next one, as yet unknown. I no longer try to analyze this hunger; I capitulated long ago to the book lust that's afflicted me most of my life. I know enough about the course of the disease to know I'll discover something soon.

This rainy afternoon my wife and daughter are out of the house, and I've got a few hours to kill. An odd phrase that, time to kill, when we almost always mean to bring back time, increase time, re-animate time, actually hold it more tightly. What better place to enjoy the stretched hours than a bookstore. I pop around the corner to our local store, which I've already scoured twice in the past three days, but it seems worth another try, and besides, the weather is perfect for it. I may be in the store for five minutes or an hour, it doesn't really matter. I do know that I'll leave with some book and head home to spend hours, both lost and found, in the perfect solitude of my sagging green easy chair.

I cruise my usual route through the store, past the stacked faces of new hardcovers and the wall of recent paperbacks, once around the magazines. Even though I was here yesterday morning, every day brings new arrivals, and while there's nothing startling today, there's still pleasure in looking at the same books again, wondering about that one on the history of the compass, or admiring the photograph of the moon on this novel, the bulk and sheen of all these books. I'm in a secretive mood—because of the rain, I imagine—and I'm drawn into the Fiction section by the claustrophobic air of its narrow canyon.

The other customers are evenly distributed throughout the store as if they've chosen their interests by the space around a given island of books. Everyone is holding a book. Some are reading from the text, others only the back-cover copy. I recognize one of the browsers from the neighborhood, an elderly man dressed in black and a squashed cowboy hat. He sports a thin, braided ponytail and a gray Walt Whitman beard and carries an ornate silver-knobbed cane. Today, he's flipping through the top shelf of Mythology, angling the volumes out from their neat row, quickly scanning them.

I'm enough of a book snoop to know that this man, a nodding acquaintance, usually reads either pulpy-looking Science Fiction, or Greek and Latin classics in their originals. The habit of book-snooping is, I admit, an annoying one, peering over the shoulder of the person on the bus, or at a café trying to decipher the cover of an open book someone's busy reading. There's no judgment in the titles I uncover, it's mere curiosity, for the most part, with a bit of selfishness to it. I might find what I'm looking for in the arm of a passing pedestrian.

I turn to the Fiction wall and regard the face-outs, the stacks of new and popular titles whose front covers are revealed. They're all pleasing, but nothing catches my attention, so I tilt my head to the right and follow the closely packed spines of the other novels and stories. Nothing grabs me, and I feel adrift for a moment. After seventeen years of working in bookstores, and even more, before and since, as a victim of book lust, I've gazed at millions of feet of shelf space, and I should be quite over the allure, the slight magic that's entranced me, but I'm not. I continue to graze, unappeased. And then, there it is, on the bottom shelf, the book I've been looking for the last few days, even though I didn't know it existed.

Andrei Platonov's *The Fierce and Beautiful World,* a collection of short stories. The title alone is irresistible, but it's the book itself, the object, that sways me, its beauty and feel. Platonov, I learn, was a daring Russian writer who wrote during, and against, the Soviet regime, the author of many novels and stories, a cult figure in his own lifetime. The editorial copy describes his stories as harsh fables of life in a totalitarian state. It's not a new book—it was written before WW II—and this reprint is already a few years old. *The Fierce and Beautiful World* is a thin paperback but solid, graced by a black-and-white photograph of a futurist spherical building; the title appears in a purple box with bright red and white type. The spine uses the same colors, space-age purple and red, with elegant, simple typography. I stoop to retrieve the book from the bottom shelf, dust my hand over the cover, weigh the fit in my folded palm, and open it. The pages are thick and creamy, and thumb nicely. The end papers, unusual in a paperback, are colored, that riveting purple again. I tuck the book under my arm. Sold.

But I won't leave the store just yet. Like the rest of my fellow customers, I'm happy to be here in this cozy and solid place, happy to be alone among others.

||||||

Like many book-lust sufferers, there was nothing in my past that would clearly lead me to my obsession with books and bookstores. I grew up in San Jose, California, a prosperous though decidedly unliterary suburb fifty miles south of San Francisco. In the early 1970s, when I was in high school, San Jose did not boast any world-class bookstore—no City Lights, no Shakespeare and Co., no Blackwell's, no Strand—but there were bookstores.

I became a voracious reader and book luster at fifteen, after discovering *The Grapes of Wrath*. For several years, I cared little about a store's atmosphere or reputation; I was concerned only that it carried books.

When I wanted new books, I hung out at the local B. Dalton located in the dark basement of our biggest shopping center, or at a tiny Little Professor tucked into the back end of a nearby strip mall. I bought mass-market editions of Steinbeck (every single one within six months), Cheever, Updike (for the respectable naughty bits), Vonnegut, Heller, Barth, Barthelme, Pynchon. I read with no particular aim or agenda and allowed the blurbs on the back of one cheap paperback to lead me to the next.

Each Thursday night, I accompanied my mother to the Valley Fair mall, and while she was getting her hair done, I'd wander to the neighboring department store's book section, where I purchased my first hardcover, the Modern Library's *Complete Tales of Saki*. I knew nothing about Saki except that it was a pseudonym (a fact irresistible to a teenager), but I loved the red and blue and green cloth covers of the Modern Library, and Saki was the cheapest at $2.95. A year earlier, I'd shoplifted a book from this same store, a hardcover copy of *Lennon*

Remembers, tucking the book into the large pocket of my brother's Marine Corps field jacket. But then, after discovering Steinbeck and the thrills of reading, I could no longer bring myself to steal a book.

I often ventured into San Jose's disheveled downtown and wandered the mazes of the cavernous used bookstores near the state college. I was ignored by the clerks while I sat for hours, skipping from book to book, with an occasional detour through the stacks of used *Playboys.*

My bookstore obsession grew to the point where I'd search for new shops during family trips, as though that were the reason for our travel. In cities up and down California, I came across stores—in Monterey, San Francisco, Santa Barbara, Los Angeles, Berkeley—where the atmosphere was markedly different from my neighborhood haunts. In these stores books were not treated as mere commodity, and there was a palpable sense of reverence for books and the time it took to read them. Since this was the 1970s, such reverence was often made evident through the decor—dark, rough paneling, potted ferns, and faded tapestries. For the last two years of high school I was unaware that such a place, Upstart Crow and Co. Bookstore and Coffeehouse, had opened a short bike ride from my home. I had to trip over it to find it, and when I did, I was trying to impress a date.

Upstart Crow was located in the Pruneyard, a rambling, two-story, upscale outdoor mall done up in neo-Spanish colonial style, with flowery, covered walkways, tiled fountains, a fake bell tower, and terra-cotta roofs. The Pruneyard painted shopping as a leisurely stroll, a perfect California day of spending, and I'd heard it was quite the place for impressing a date. Mine was no ordinary date; I was with the fair Selinda, and yet it became increasingly hard to maintain my teenage cool after stumbling upon this cave of wonders.

Decades ahead of other book retailers, Upstart Crow's owners had created something of a theme park, where the atmosphere (I'm sure they thought of it as "ambience") was as much a draw as the merchandise. There were foreign periodicals, chessboards, plenty of big tables and comfy chairs, and summoning the tradition of the English coffeehouse—shades of Dr. Johnson, *The Tatler*, those who made the eighteenth-century coffeehouse an institution—Upstart Crow brought the first espresso bar to our neck of the woods.

The walls of this coffeehouse and bookstore were covered with framed prints and photographs of writers who were surely famous, even though I had not yet heard of them: Geoffrey Chaucer, Rudyard Kipling, Virginia Woolf, Edith Sitwell, Graham Greene, E. M. Forster (who for some reason appeared in his photo in drag as Queen Victoria), and dozens of others, mostly British. Typed labels identified the writers, and I whispered these names aloud to remember them. There was a close sense of history in this brand-new place, a sense of the importance of the past and its legacy, a sense of history I found remarkable, growing up as I had in past-less California.

What struck me most, however, was that these famous writers lived on. Their photos were more than decor; their books stocked the store's shelves.

The name of the store was enough to make me feel connected to a past I could as yet only intuit. The Upstart Crow is Shakespeare, so named by an envious contemporary of the Bard, Rob't Greene, who wrote,

> yet trust them not: for there is an Upstart Crow,
> beautified with our feathers, that with his Tygers
> Hart wrapt in a Players hyde, supposes he is as
> well able to bombast out a blank verse as the
> best of you . . .

The quote appeared on the store's bookmarks, along with a Leonard Baskin drawing of a crow. I *knew* it: here was proof that there were people in the world, adults who weren't high school teachers, who understood the importance of Shakespeare and books and writing.

I still have one of those bookmarks, along with a few other things from Crow, a captain's chair and a plain white coffee mug, both of which I stole after four years of happy employment. But I don't have the orange book bag with the perfect-length shoulder strap. That, and much else, has been lost.

It was more than the atmosphere that grabbed me. There were the usual stacks of beautifully photographed and reasonably priced cat books, and rows of mass-market Self-Help and Romance, but also stacks of books by the writers whose photos graced the walls, and many others, all engagingly displayed. The books I'd sought in other stores were always stuffed into a far corner or downstairs, but here every book was promoted. I wandered the shelves and tables with a gape-mouthed reverence, gravitating to the S's in Fiction, where I found a book that I had already purchased and read, but whose present incarnation amazed me.

The Long Valley was one of my favorite Steinbecks, mine was a tiny mass-market edition. Upstart Crow carried a Viking Compass edition, a trade paperback with beautiful type and a serious, Expressionist cover. This edition made me feel the power of its words before I'd turned to the first page.

Selinda and I sat in the coffee bar, sipping Café Mit Schlag, a drink I ordered for its name and which thankfully came festooned with whipped cream. On the way out that night, I paid for *The Long Valley* at the front counter and asked for a job application.

IIIIII

It's a good thing bookstores are places for hanging out, spending more time than money, because Upstart Crow didn't hire me for nearly two years, although not for lack of trying on my part. I was there nearly every week, as if I might be hired by sheer obstinance, and three times I filled out an application, which was a written test of literary knowledge. The first time I took the test I missed only one question: What category of books does Donna

Meilach write? (Arts and Crafts). Charlotte, the manager, was always friendly but leery of hiring a high school student. The summer after my freshman year of college, Charlotte brought me on for temporary help with shelving, finally tired, I imagine, of listening to my wheedling. I was so certain I'd be taken on permanently, I left a thriving career as a 7-Eleven Slurpee jockey.

During my first week at Crow, I did nothing but shelve box upon box of Penguin paperbacks. At first I was hesitant, ferrying small handfuls of green, black, and orange books from one wrong section to another, but soon I was arm-loading twenty to thirty at a time, all now broken down by subject and precisely alphabetized. I was thrilled by the weighty order of the books, and by the vast web of names and titles I did not know; this may have been the moment when I realized there would never be enough time in my life to read everything.

At the end of that first week, passing the new hardcover releases, I happened upon a book that would not let me go, John Steinbeck's *The Acts of King Arthur and His Noble Knights,* a posthumous work, recently published, with a cover in imitation of an illuminated manuscript, deckled (or rough) pages on the fore-edge, maroon cloth under the dust jacket, and perfectly pristine. I had read every Steinbeck in existence, and knew, I thought, all there was to be know on the subject, so such a book seemed impossible to me. And there were five copies! Charlotte tried to talk me out of buying it, and she was right; I would have to shelve for five hours to pay for it, even with my discount. One of the other clerks, Greta Ray, came up next to me, stroked the book lightly with the palm of her hand, and said, "It really is beautiful, isn't it?" It was beautiful, so I bought it.

I knew that I had found what I could only describe then as a cool job, although the feeling was more profound and complex. I felt as if I had found the proper city in which to dwell. What I knew that day, what drew me to the bookstore, I would not be able to articulate for many years. But my inability to describe the feeling did nothing to diminish its power over me. Books, I knew then and now, give body to our ideas and imaginations, make them flesh in the world; a bookstore is the city where our fleshed-out inner selves reside.

While I shelved the last of that day's shipment, the books appeared like a city's lighted windows, seductive glimpses of the lives that dwelled between their covers. This was more than retail, this was pleasure, both intangible and sensual. I also sensed that the customers and clerks who wandered the streets of this city were like-minded souls, who believed that the book and what it held were one and the same, both common and rare.

Leaving at dusk that day, I stopped to say good night to Greta. She was sitting behind the long front counter, against the tall windows that looked out on the covered walkway and the parking lot. She asked to see Steinbeck's *King Arthur* again, and cooed over it. "Goddamn it," she said. "It *is* beautiful." We stood there talking for the longest time.

‖‖‖

Greta Ray was a complete surprise to me, certainly the type of person I'd never expected to meet. She was close to my mother's age, I knew that, late generation World War II, but far from the stereotypical housewife of my limited experience. I would have called Greta a hippie then, in 1976, with all of that word's positive connotations, but bohemian might be more apt. I had grown up in a military family, traditional and working class; Greta had lived the kind of life I thought existed only in books.

She had short peppery hair, the reddish complexion and angular beauty of a native American, and startling blue eyes. She wore the authentic hippie attire of northern California: blue jeans, sometimes with patches; peasant blouses; Birkenstocks before they got a bad rap. She also wore funky pieces of silver jewelry her husband made for her out of pre-war Australian quarters. Her husband, Jack, was a professor of logic, a writer, painter, and flutist. I learned they had met in beachside L.A. in the late 1940s, part of a glamorous crowd into jazz and sports cars. They had smoked marijuana in the fifties and were early opponents of the war in Vietnam. They were thrilled to be in the audience when Dylan went electric. Their children attended a very alternative school called Daybreak. Real paintings hung in their house, among them Jack's "Logicians Dancing." Greta thought the Kinks were the greatest rock band in the world.

She was also the most learned, voracious reader I had ever met, and while raising her kids, and helping to write and edit Jack's papers, Greta worked in bookstores.

Her first job was at Buffum's Department Store in Long Beach, California, in 1949. She had been working across the street at a music store, but visited Buffum's basement lending library so often they finally gave her a job. She had also worked at Smith's Acres of Books, Iowa Book and Supply, Kit's, and later, Printer's Inc. She'd been at Upstart Crow for five years when I met her.

Greta and I had talked a couple of times when I was still a customer at the store. During my freshman year in college, I discovered a first book of stories by the still unknown Raymond Carver. I borrowed and devoured *Will You Please Be Quiet, Please?* from the college library, and unable to find the book elsewhere in San Jose over winter break, I special ordered it from Greta, who knew the book and talked at length about this writer I assumed I alone had discovered.

Later, when I started at Crow, after having served my time as a temporary shelving apprentice (something akin to a cabin boy), my head now filled with thousands of new titles and authors, I was rewarded with regular shifts and began to spend more time with Greta, who taught me about the cash register, the inventory system, customer service and special orders, the proper way to display a table or stuff a shelf, and it would turn out, much that was not included in the employee handbook.

||||||

For the first couple of years, Greta and I worked the night shift, which is a different country indeed. We'd arrive at

four in the afternoon and leave near midnight after closing and cleaning up. Most of the ordering and shelving
was done by the day managers, and for the two clerks on
the night shift, the task was to keep the store open and
running. Without the busier work, we had time to enjoy
the space.

The coffee bar was set into the back of the brightly
lit bookshop, and behind it, lay the darker grotto of the
coffeehouse's constellation of tables. I always dropped
into work early to scoot behind the bar for a cup of
Sumatra, chatting with the barristas, students like myself,
but whose style tended to be punkier than the bookstore
staff's—dyed hair, multiple earrings, thrift-store black. I'd
chat with some of the regulars at the bar and peer into
the coffeehouse to see who might be back there, maybe
Chess Guy or Tarot Lady. A lot of regulars came in every
day for months or years at a stretch. They came at prescribed times, stayed for hours, and while we might talk
to them daily, we might never know their real names.
The most regular of the regulars at this time was Zoltan,
a thirtyish fellow of seemingly independent means, who
spent seven or eight hours a day in the coffeehouse. He
kept undisclosed notes in a fat binder and was inclined
to discuss issues of social philosophy rather than the
weather. Zoltan was still an everyday fixture at Crow
when the store closed ten years later, and we can only
assume he found a new home-away-from-home.

There were also the drop-ins and the semi-regulars,
all seated at the wrought-iron and wood tables in cap-

tain's chairs or rattan thrones. Dim spotlights, heaps of open books and newspapers, a rather lazy mood to it all. The bookstore and the coffeehouse are natural allies; neither has a time limit, slowness is encouraged.

On her stool behind the front counter in the evenings, Greta would be going through the special orders, sipping her coffee, smoking a never-ending cigarette, and cursing the inability of most of humanity to fill out a simple form. We'd play records we'd brought in from home; Greta took me through the jazz catalogue to start with, my first tastes of Miles, Coltrane, Bird. We'd ring up a few customers, answer the phone, enjoy the lull.

Coffee finished, I'd wander off to straighten the store, a perpetual chore (although Sisyphus never had it this good), and by the start of the evening rush, the store was tamed and ordered, all possibility, ready to get trashed again.

The rest of the shift was devoted to helping people find books. A simple enough proposition, mind you, and frequently customers did have the exact information and only needed to be guided to the proper shelf and alphabet. At other times, finding the right title could be like constructing an ancient religion from a single artifact. Who could guess that *Roger the Sorcerer* was code for *Roget's Thesaurus?*

No matter how roundabout the path, it's always satisfying to put the right book in the right hands, but the real thrill in bookselling is to put the right book into unsuspecting hands. Because I found her name enchanting,

I still remember Victoria McIlvrag, one of the first customers I ever surprised with a book. Today I don't remember much about her, except that she wore a brown raincoat and was always with her young son. The first time we met, she told me she had been reading nothing but trashy best sellers—her words—and she loved to read but wanted something new; she wanted to read about real women. I led her to Fiction and handed her a blue and silver copy of Eudora Welty's *The Optimist's Daughter.* Ms. McIlvrag looked at the book with some skepticism, but bought it anyway, and came back the next week asking for more by Ms. Welty, please, and anything else I cared to recommend.

After the rush, Greta and I would redo the shelves for the last hour or so, then close the store at eleven, and draw ourselves a glass of Anchor Steam beer before we counted and deposited the money. We would sweep and clean, yelling to each other across the loud music we played, Neil Young or Genesis or whatever album we'd discovered that week.

On one of those first nights, after closing, listening to Getz and Gilberto, Greta presented me with three books, and said sternly, "Now, goddamn it, Lewis, be quiet and listen to me. You have to read these books, and that's all there is to it." She gave me William Faulkner's *The Sound and the Fury, The Essays of E.B. White,* and *Higglety Pigglety Pop* by Maurice Sendak. Just like that, three entire worlds opened up for me, and thirty years later I'm still reading these writers, their worlds still moving through me. "Besides," she said then, pointing to the books, "just look at them, they're gorgeous."

The coffeehouse was shut up, the parking lot a tundra, and Greta and I often stayed too late, loading new records, jumping from one section to another with books in hand, our enthusiasms wagging their furry tails. We were quite happy there, alone together among our books.

The conversation we began that night has continued for thirty years now. Greta and I worked together forty hours a week for the first ten years—four years at Upstart Crow and six at Printers Inc. in Palo Alto. She saw me through my education, my first marriage, my first madness, the subsequent madnesses, my second marriage, the birth of my daughter. At various junctures I've lived with Greta and her family, sleeping on the couch or floor. We've mourned her husband, her dearest friend, and her youngest son. While our friendship has gone well beyond our love of books, that love has always been central, and at least for us, it's impossible to find any boundary between books and life in the world. Today, we see each other maybe six times a year, but talk on the phone once or twice a week. When she calls, it's always morning and she's already breathless. "Have you read . . ?"

What Greta was trying to tell me that night, and ever since, was that the books are right, we are not alone.

The Magic Box

No child sets out to become a bookseller. Before the onset of my book lust, I had wanted, variously, to be an astronaut, a deep-sea diver, an astronomer, a football player, a Marine sergeant, a stand-up comic, and a rock star. The image most people have of the profession—the bookseller seated on a stool with a nice volume of Jane Austen, drinking tea and patting the cat—is cozy, perhaps, but far short of glamour and heroics. Fortunately or otherwise, we are not in charge of where our lives will take us; not all of us become firemen.

The turning moments in my life have often felt at the time accidental, random, but when I look back, with the perspective of my years, I find that there were always signposts pointing to my destination. At twelve, hearing the Beatles's *Abbey Road* was a huge curveball for me. Where did such sounds come from, how were they created, and why had I found Bobby Goldsboro's sappy ballad "Honey" so stimulating only a week before? My first listening of *Abbey Road* changed the way I saw the entire world and my place in it—good-bye football player, hello rock star. But it wasn't until a book report in my sophomore year of high school that I discovered the power of words and was overcome by the urge to read. Still, hadn't the Beatles in some way prepared me for Steinbeck by opening my imagination of the world?

When I started working at Upstart Crow, I took to bookselling with a passion that surprised me. No mere college job, this would be my life's occupation. The choice seemed mysterious, as if I'd been anointed, called.

Many years later, a stray memory helped me find another childhood root of my passion for bookselling. One of the true pleasures of my elementary school life was Scholastic's *Weekly Reader*, a newspaper distributed free to classrooms around the country. It featured brief articles on current events, sports, and nature, along with jokes, puzzles, and cartoons. The *Weekly Reader* was a wholly satisfying reading experience, whose joy was, in part, the unexpected ownership of the publication; I was stunned to be allowed such a privilege. The ultimate delight of the *Weekly Reader,* however, lay in ordering and receiving my very own books from a catalogue appended to the newspaper. This catalogue, as I remember it, was four pages on newspaper stock, two-color printing with black-and-white photographs of the books' covers. On *Weekly Reader* days I'd spend a good deal of our reading hour—languorous late afternoons of twenty-two buzzy, dreamy heads bent over words, the teacher nearly asleep—scanning the catalogue, looking for standout cover art, titles that promised magic, mystery, sometimes war. When I finished my first go-through, ritual dictated I return to the first page and slowly read each synopsis, weighing the many possibilities.

By dinner that evening, I would have made my choices, the three or four books I was allowed at twenty-five or thirty-five cents each, the latter more expensive because thicker. I'd mark the order form with the thickest of X's, so there'd be no mistakes, cut along the dotted line, and put it in an envelope with the coins my parents helped me count out. The next day I'd clank the order on the teacher's desk, then wait for the books to arrive. And wait. Four to six weeks is several eternities for a nine-year-old.

The books finally did arrive. Not as if by magic, but as if by design; someone knew exactly when I'd forget about the books, and that's when they'd arrive. I'd turn my head to stare out the classroom window at a fat robin in the grass, and when I looked back, the box would be sitting on the teacher's desk. The teacher would slice through the packing tape with the opened blade of her scissors and pull out bundles of books rubber-banded together with the order forms. Finally, my bundle would emerge from the box, and the afternoon would be given over to the thin, bright paperbacks, their woody smell and sleek covers. *Radar Commandos, Murder by Moonlight, Mystery Under the Sea, Brighty of the Grand Canyon, Follow My Leader, Misty of Chincoteague.* I would rarely get any reading done on this day; the books themselves were enough. The last bell would ring, and I'd race home.

At Upstart Crow, and in each bookstore after that, I've always been thrilled by the arrival of boxes of books, and on opening those boxes, the goods that would spill out. I've never tired of this, and even when I visit a bookstore today, I'm drawn to the stacks of boxes that clutter the aisles—hey, you need a hand with those? This compulsion of mine, I'm convinced, is tied to the *Weekly Reader* and Miss Baab's fourth-grade classroom and the lazy wonder of those afternoons.

At her school, my daughter receives the same catalogues—seven or eight at a time, each a different reading level—and she and I spend hours choosing preliminary candidates, painfully making the final selection, which she marks with her thickest X's. Much to my relief, her teachers don't open the boxes in front of the kids, the book orders simply appear in the student cubbies. I'm hoping this sleight of hand might save her from the penury of a bookseller's life.

||||||

When the "need to read" first hit me, it seemed a sudden accident in my life, one that puzzled me for a long time. I believed myself set apart from the others in my family, different, therefore better. Like others, I had occasionally hoped, sometimes prayed, that I had been adopted, or purchased from a roguish gypsy family that might someday return for me.

When Greta and I were first working together, I was a sophomore in college—both literally and figuratively—

and I used to wonder aloud how I'd been selected out of all my family to be the one who was going to . . . the one who was obviously . . . well, what exactly I didn't know, only that it was better. My parents only read, I'd tell Greta, lesser literature. While I had become . . . elevated, enlightened? My preening finally wore Greta out, and one day she called me on it. We were standing in the middle of the store, alphabetizing a section that had been ignored for a while, probably Business.

"Lewis," she said. "You are so full of shit. Who do you think you are?"

I knew enough to pay attention when Greta spoke to me in this tone. She asked me if my parents read. They did, but. . . . My mother read Gothic novels, tons of them, over and over, zooming through one a night. My father mostly read periodicals, the *San Jose Mercury, Time*, as well as *Argosy* and *True*, men's adventures magazines once found in all barbershops. I tried to explain to Greta how trite this reading matter was, that is, nothing *I* would ever read, but she insisted I ought to be thankful.

Parents didn't have to read the *New York Review of Books* or James Joyce, and they didn't have to make their kids read *Treasure Island* or Greek myths. Parents simply had to read for themselves, and to make sure there were kids' books in the house. Children had only to see that reading was something adults did for pleasure and, following this example, would begin to read on their own.

Greta also taught me that being too prescriptive, or proscriptive, in a child's reading choices, can be harmful. Let children find their own pleasure in reading. At Printers Inc., where Greta and I worked after Crow, a store situated near the Stanford University campus, an area where academic pressures on children are very high, a couple came in one day and asked me to choose several "classics" for their eleven-year-old daughter. She loved to read, they said, it was practically all she did, but she read only "trash." At the time she was consumed by *The Babysitters' Club,* an endless series of formulaic novels about a group of charmingly average "tweener" girls. The couple wanted their daughter to read more seriously, *Treasure Island* or Dickens. I was showing them what we had, when I noticed their daughter nearby, seated on the floor in front of the shelf where we kept *The Babysitters' Club.* She was poring over the newest book in the series, reading as fast as she possibly could the only book she really wanted. I hope I remember correctly that, along with *Ivanhoe* that day, they also bought number 37 in the *Babysitter* series.

||||||

I was not a particularly voracious or literary reader as a child, not one of those kids who read Dickens under the bedcovers by flashlight, who had to have the book snatched from their hands at the dinner table, or who dreamed of flying-books to read while walking. But the path to my "need to read" was laid out for me in the most important ways. That is, my parents had done all the work.

My mother had planned to go to college, but was derailed by meeting my father and WWII; and my father, a sharecropper's son, had left school after eighth grade. Children of the Great Depression, they were determined that their children have every opportunity for an education.

In our quiet living room (as opposed to the TV-centered family room) was a long shelf of books: novels, including *Reader's Digest* condensed novels and selections from the Family Book Club, suitable for all ages; some biography and history and science (Jacques Cousteau's *The Silent World,* on my bookshelf today); a family Bible, the dates of the dead and the living inscribed on the endpapers; a cumbersome dictionary; and a colorful atlas, whose pink and green and yellow countries often led me to stare out the window and dream of faraway lands.

My parents also purchased, at the county fair the summer I turned five, a set of the World Book Encyclopedia in its own special bookcase, and which was, I remember, a real stretch for our budget. Contrary to the popular notion, kids do use the encyclopedia for reasons other than book reports, though the World Book certainly did get a workout during report season; Father Junipero Serra, Brazil, and Vermont are report topics that spring to mind. But I also spent many long hours on the scratchy green carpet in our living room, leafing from subject to subject, having gone to the encyclopedia for one piece of information, *Dirigible,* say, and ending up in the middle of *Dunkirk,* alphabetically just below that, or moving on to *Hydrogen* as prompted by the key-word highlighting.

My parents, taking turns, read to me each night from *The Tall Book of Fairy Tales* and the Volland edition of *Great Children's Stories,* new editions of which I read to my own daughter. The pleasure for Maddy in these stories must be so different than mine. She is hearing them for the first time and must find the illustrations startling. I see and hear the stories through a filter of memory's movements, the stories familiar to so many generations—"Jack and the Beanstalk," "Three Billy Goat's Gruff," "The Bremen Town Musicians." The illustrations evoke for me those distant nights, suddenly near, spent close to my mother and father, tucked safe in bed, the day ordered, punctuated, by the telling of a story, my parents whispering later, "Blow out the light." As I whisper now to my daughter.

My mother has been preserving boxes of my childhood world all these years and is slowly returning bits of that world to me, for which I'm grateful. The books that have come down to me aren't the classics, but a random selection of titles that have been mostly forgotten. Among those she's kept alive are some Little Elf books from the travel publisher Rand McNally, and while I remember the books, I find the travel themes in them to be close to propaganda. *Muggins Takes Off* is about a rather saccharine mouse who hops a ride aboard a Mercury space flight; *Volksy the Little Yellow Car* makes a lovable character out of the first compact-sized automobile in the United States; and *Choo-Choo The Little Switch Engine* is a parable on the efficiency of the railroad. Despite the limited appeal of these books over the ages, I'm nonetheless captured by their hastily drawn landscapes—the snowy farm road, the clover-dense meadow—and I fall into these worlds again, not as much for the enchantment, but for the familiarity. I loved those books then, and my daughter likes them now.

My parents frequently bought us books, as whim and reward, but mostly from book outlets in venues other than bookstores, especially from Woolworth's (ah, the scent of the popcorn there, or a counter lunch of grilled cheese and chocolate shakes) where I picked up, from among the jumbo crossword treasuries, a number of cheap hardcovers based on TV shows and sports—*Dragnet, I Spy, Man from U.N.C.L.E., The Long Bomb, The Grand Slam.* We also bought books at Gemco department stores and Rexall Drug.

Almost every time I bought a book in one of these stores it's because my mother was in the book section, too, picking up several of her Gothic novels—Phyllis Whitney, Victoria Holt—precursors to contemporary romances, though much thinner, and the covers were usually dour blacks and grays rather than pinks and crimsons. Instead of showing women swept away by brawny men with fabulous hair, the covers portrayed lone women wrapped in shawls and standing on the edge of storm-tossed cliffs. Still the same plot: woman in trouble, saved by man. My mother had read so many of these novels that occasionally she'd find herself in the middle of one, only to realize she'd read it before.

There were libraries, of course, and I often visited my local branch, a squat Modernist building with no sign of a front door. I still have a keen sense of windy, shaded afternoons and the stacks of plastic-wrapped books, the qualifying ker-chunk of the date stamp, my own library card with its wobbly signature. And the one-room library of my junior high school and its high-up windows, where the librarian chose for me two seminal books: *The Teddy Bear Habit,* about a boy, his Teddy Bear, and Ed Sullivan; and *The Strawberry Statement,* a diary of the Berkeley free-speech movement. The problem with libraries, I discovered, was that two weeks later, I'd have to load up the bike and, with a sense of loss, return the books.

Mostly, I stuck to my Scholastic books—*Encyclopedia Brown, The Mad Scientist's Club, Homer Price, The Big Book of Tricks and Projects.* On occasion I'd pick something that looked classy, *Huckleberry Finn* or an abridged *Rise and Fall of the Third Reich.* Nothing too heavy, mind you, and not too much of it, because there was a lot of TV to watch and a lot of bike to ride.

The books of our childhood offer a vivid door to our own pasts, and not necessarily for the stories we read there, but for the memories of where we were and who we were when we were reading them; to remember a book is to remember the child who read that book. My aunt Mimi gave me a child's introduction to archaeology when I was six, and coming upon that book now, I am taken back to my bedroom on Flood Drive in San Jose, reading in bed at night, and the precise moment when I understood that the written word "says" was pronounced "sez" rather than rhyming with the plural of "hay." I can see the brown cowboy bedspread, lariats and corrals rampant, feel the orange-tasseled fringe of it, and know again the child I was. Find an old book from your childhood, take a good whiff, and suddenly you're living Proust.

There's nothing exceptional in my reading history, and that's why I've chosen to detail it. For those who are afflicted with book lust, those for whom reading is more than information or escape, the road to our passion is quite simple, paved merely by the presence of printed matter.

It's a common story; fill in your own blanks: I was _____ years old when I happened on a novel called _____, and within six months I had read every other book by the writer known as _____.

I was fifteen. *The Grapes of Wrath.* John Steinbeck.

‖‖‖‖

I still have my first copy of *The Grapes of Wrath*, a cracked, taped-together thing I stole from Mrs. Jouthas's American Lit. class because I couldn't bear to part with it, and because of my crush on Mrs. Jouthas. I did, however, out of guilt and a sense of the book's value, pay for a replacement copy.

Today, one sniff of that book's cheap pulpy paper takes me back to that class: an entire year of wishing that Cheri Miller would finally see how cool I was, a year of trading snide remarks with Diana Tucker, who would work with me at Upstart Crow some years later and is someone I still trade snide remarks with today. I can see the posters above Mrs. Jouthas's blackboard— Onomatopoeia, "the bells, bells, bells"; and Metonymy, "football is king"—and see her immaculate handwriting in blue, green, and yellow chalks. That was more than thirty years ago.

My most powerful reading memory is the opening chapter of *The Grapes of Wrath.* Night again, a different bedspread, olive green with traffic signs, Beatles posters on the wall, Cream on the record player. I had come to the book in a roundabout way, through my cousin Chuck, fourteen years older, who was living with us while attending graduate school in business. He'd suggested *The Grapes of Wrath,* saying I must read it or forever be doomed to a life of long hair and Dr Pepper, and because he seemed so wise, I took it up, though with some pain. It seemed very long. But it was time to get started on the book report, and lying on my bed in the privacy of that teenage night, I cracked open the first pages, completely unprepared: "To the red country and part of the gray country of Oklahoma, the last rains came gently, and they did not cut the scarred earth."

When I typed these lines from memory, I was surprised at how well I did; I spelled "gray" with an "e," and omitted "part of" and one comma.

By the time I finished the first chapter, I was determined that I, too, would be a writer someday, and that I would read everything else by Mr. Steinbeck, who I discovered, to my chagrin, had died six years earlier. I interrupted my reading long enough to write the first pages of my first short story, then went back to Steinbeck, and read until dawn.

I believe every compulsive reader has an ideal reading spot; mine is the orange Naugahyde recliner in my childhood living room. My latchkey afternoons became devoted to hours of reading in that chair, the close autumn sun pouring richly over the white paperback, its black spine, and dyed yellow edges. When I finished with *The Grapes of Wrath*, I stayed in that chair, and started in on *Cannery Row*, and every two or three days, I'd bicycle across the flat suburbia of the Santa Clara Valley to a tiny B. Dalton store to purchase another Steinbeck with the money I made washing dishes at a card club. Then it was back to the big chair.

As a typically lonely American teenager, who preferred my noises and company on the loud side, these afternoons were a revelation to me: the joy of solitude, the pleasure of it. I remember these newly consuming afternoons and the books I held there as much as what I read, but I remember the afternoons because of what I read. Steinbeck's words, and those of the writers who followed, took me out of my San Jose self and transported me to new worlds. In the course of one week, ensconced in the big chair, I might travel to Kenya or Peru, enjoy the decadence of an English manor, or get shipped to the Gulag; I could be man or woman, child or ghost.

|||||||

It isn't only the surprise of the exotic that first draws us into books, it's also the recognition we feel. My friend Liz Szabla was fourteen when she discovered Ernest Hemingway and cut school one day to stay home and finish *A Farewell to Arms,* which she'd started the night before, another fortuitous book report. There's a lot of vermouth in *A Farewell to Arms,* and Liz was so captured by the book that she raided her mother's liquor cabinet: lo and behold, vermouth. She poured herself a milk tumbler's worth, settled into the big chair in her family room, and spent the day sipping and reading, slightly tipsy, and occasionally pounding the arm of the chair, yelling to the empty house, "Yes, yes, that's the way it is, yes, yes, yes, he knows everything, exactly, I love this book." Liz lost track of the time and did not hear her mother's key in the door. Her mother wasn't so much angry with Liz as surprised that anyone had the perseverance to drink that much "dry" vermouth. Hemingway's characters, of course, were drinking "sweet" vermouth, slightly more palatable.

Reading alone in her chair, Liz felt the first great stir of connecting with a world beyond her own: she drank vermouth and felt deeply in tune with Lieutenant Henry and Miss Barkley in the streets of Milan, the war booming in the nearby mountains. Not only was there a big world out there, Liz knew she belonged in it and knew in her bones that there were others like her.

The strangeness and the recognition of reading are almost always mingled, and I first encountered their confluence in a visceral way. While much of the setting for *The Grapes of Wrath,* California's central valley, was only a few hours from San Jose, it might as well have been the moon to me; I had come from Okie stock on my father's side, but the plight of the Joads was yet science fiction. After *The Grapes of Wrath,* I read Steinbeck's other California fiction—*East of Eden, Cannery Row, Tortilla Flat, The Long Valley* and others—all set in the Salinas Valley and on the Monterey coast an hour's drive from San Jose. The landscape that Steinbeck described with loving power, the soft steep coastal hills, "shaded and dusky," and the live oak and manzanita forests, was a landscape I knew, but through his prose, I came to see this world, my only world then, as if for the first time, and I would ride my bike into the hills to see them for myself but with Steinbeck's words still tumbling in me. Finally, it seemed to me, I knew the names of the world, names that had always been just out of reach like late-summer apricots on the highest branches.

When I turned sixteen, and *finally* got my driver's license, I would get in the car, cutting school, and drive down to Steinbeck country to roam and wonder. My favorite spot on these trips was Cannery Row, at that time a tacky strip of art galleries and abandoned sardine canneries that still spoke of Steinbeck's world: rotted-out boilers, run-down "paisano" shacks, vacant lots carpeted with lime green sweetgrass. I'd nose around the salt-worn laboratory of Doc Ricketts, Steinbeck's closest friend, through whose cracked windows I spied specimen jars of squid, anemone, and frogs, which perhaps Steinbeck himself had helped catch and prepare. Across the street was Wing Fat's, the Chinese grocer where the locals once bought pints of "old Tennis Shoes," and just up the hill, Flora's, the local brothel, now, to my disappointment, a cheap spaghetti restaurant. I'd perch on a piling above the tide pools and stare at the ocean for hours, here in a very real place where vivid, yet imaginary characters wandered.

I'd been to Cannery Row before I discovered Steinbeck, but had only seen it as a place with a nice view of the ocean. Now, through Steinbeck's musings on Robert Louis Stevenson, one of his favorite boyhood writers, I knew that I was standing at the edge of the Western world, at the end of history, looking west into the east, toward the future. The world was bigger because of Steinbeck, but also within my grasp.

IIIIII

John Steinbeck has always been a controversial writer. More of his works have been banned than those of nearly any other American writer in the last sixty years.

During his lifetime, he was spurned by the people of the Salinas Valley and driven from the place he loved most, although these days, Salinas trumpets him proudly in search of tourist dollars. He was frequently denigrated by the New York literary establishment (on his receipt of the Nobel Prize, the *New York Times* ran an op-ed on his unworthiness for such an award), and to this day his books receive a polite if mixed bag of critical assessments: too simplistic, too raw, not modern enough, certainly not postmodern nor postironic. And yet, since the publication of *The Grapes of Wrath* in 1939, his books have remained in print, and his oeuvre is still among the best-selling of all time.

We do not claim a writer's excellence based on sales and popularity; there are too many books that sell millions of copies, which will not be read fifty, much less five, years from now. I've been rereading Steinbeck over the last two years (which I began with trepidation, knowing I might find my adolescent shine tarnished), and his books still surprise me with their depth and riveting clarity. But there is one indisputable assessment we can make of Steinbeck, placing him in a category that's often overlooked in literary and cultural histories. Steinbeck's books are important because they are formative ones. They often spark in younger readers a longing to know more about the world, to engage, and to continue reading. Maybe the proper term for such work is books of engagement.

Books like Steinbeck's spur the young reader to do

more than read, spur the reader into the world. Steinbeck's Ur-book was Malory's *Le Morte D'Arthur*. These tales of chivalry not only made Steinbeck want to be a writer but also formed the core sensibility of his writing, a mythic approach to the story and the world it describes (and it's this sensibility and its intention, I think, that most critics forget when evaluating his novels and stories).

When Ronald Reagan was eleven, he was profoundly moved by a contemporary Christian allegory, *That Printer of Udele's* by Harold Bell Wright. In the novel, the hero Dick Falkner organizes a community organization to help the less fortunate, and at the novel's end, heads off to Washington, D.C., to bring his vision to the national stage. Reagan was so moved by the book that when he was finished he went directly to his mother and informed her that he was going to do the same. Reagan also became a great storyteller, first as a radio announcer, later as president. An important book, it seems, does not have to be one universally judged great or memorable.

The list of important books is long and ragged, as broad in style and subject as could be, from children's chapter books to novels we think of as literary and novels we think of as somewhat less than literary. What seems to be the common thread in these books is that they present a vivid and entire world in a fashion that's accessible to young minds, say, twelve to eighteen, but without condescension.

Greta Ray grew up in Montebello, in east Los Angeles, in a house that had previously belonged to a retired railroad man who used bits and pieces of old railcars to add a back bedroom. The bedroom had a sleeping berth, a sliding closet door taken from a W.C. (complete with the sign, "Passengers will please refrain from flushing the toilet when in the station"), a pew seat from third class, and a dining table that converted into a bed. Greta's parents owned a restaurant, and so she spent a lot of time alone, hours in the berth or the dining-table bed, apart from the world and yet part of it. What were her most important books? Nancy Drew mysteries, *Gone with the Wind,* and a hulking anthology, *Twenty-Five Tales of the Weird and Supernatural.* Not Faulkner, not Proust, but Nancy Drew; the first rungs on the ladder are often the most daring. To get to Faulkner, start with Nancy Drew. Or books about horses. Books by Kurt Vonnegut, or Ayn Rand, or *A Wrinkle in Time,* or *On the Road,* or *To Kill a Mockingbird,* or *Goosebumps.* It's entirely possible that some of tomorrow's voracious readers will cite the Harry Potter novels as important, but just as many might cite a novel not found in every house on the planet.

I'm always asking friends and acquaintances which are their formative books, and one thing I've discovered about such books, perhaps the only constant, is that when asked to name them, the ones that launched their book lust, people almost always respond with a certain embarrassment. "Oh, you know," they'll say, "just a bunch of those silly horse books." But what travel those imaginary horses provide.

The most important qualification of all, however, is that the book be compelling enough to draw the reader into the erotic space of reading, where the mind is enflamed and the body in repose. Why such transformations occur in teenagers so often seems clear; adolescence is an erotic adventure. John Irving has described adolescence as the time when we begin to keep secrets from those we love; in that secret place, we begin to find ourselves and how we might make our way in the world with that self. Take someone who likes to read; give her a comfy place to do so and ample time for doing it; add one good book, and then more; stand back.

Reading is a solitary act, but one that demands connection to the world, and while not all book lusters go into bookselling, Greta, Liz, myself, and others were drawn to the bookstore by the books that moved us, and stopping for just a moment, we each stayed for a long time.

. . . & Company

For most of my years at Upstart Crow, I was in college at a small Jesuit school whose students, in the main, were more interested in practical business degrees than in the scrutiny of English literature from Beowulf to Virginia Woolf. I knew I'd made the wiser choice of a major, English, when I saw my first-term roommate Rollie struggling with his accounting theory at the same time that I was howling with laughter over my own homework, Twain's *Life on the Mississippi*. Besides, I was getting a solid business education at Crow; I learned how to balance the accounts, monitor inventory, order and market product, develop a customer base. It was all very hands-on. But my education at Crow wasn't limited to the fundamentals of small business, nor to expanding the bibliography of everything I would have to read before I died. There were larger lessons to take in.

Soon after I joined Crow, a dinner was held at a local restaurant to celebrate Greta Ray's fifth anniversary with the company. There must have been ten of us there, members of the bookstore staff, the bookstore's managers, Donna and Charlotte, and two of the company's

owners, Ken Kitch and Kelly Cannon, both inveterate
book lusters. I was still a few years from twenty-one,
but this was 1976, things were a bit looser, and I drank
far too much wine that night, becoming even more full
of myself than usual. The talk that night was all about
books, and I was trying my best to impress the table with
all that I knew, which I assumed was pretty much all
there was to know.

I sat next to Ken Kitch that night, and he engaged me
in my ramblings. We talked about Spenser and Ariosto,
Dryden and Pope and Dr. Johnson, terza rima and ot-
tava rima. At every turn, Ken and I were trying to outdo
each other, and with Ken opposing, I was struggling to
stay afloat. A former stage-trained actor, Ken was ex-
tremely well read—as were all of Crow's owners—and
in our discussion he was as relentless as I was annoying.
But to his credit—the mentor watching out for his over-
eager pupil—he saved the crushing blow for a moment
when we were alone. The two of us were on our way
to the men's room, and I was boasting that I could recite the first eighteen lines of Chaucer's *The Canterbury
Tales.* In Middle English, no less. Go ahead, then, Ken
said. And while we stood at the urinals, I began, "Whan
that Aprill with his shoures soote . . ." I finished the
Prologue's reverdie, "That hem hath holpen what that
they were seeke," flushed, and zipped. Ken said that he
was very impressed, but did I know the next two lines?
I did not. Ken flushed, zipped, turned to me and recited,
"Biful that in that seson on a day/In Southwerk at the

Tabard as I lay," and continued for several more lines. Trumped, I returned to the table.

While the owners of Upstart Crow and Co. were ambitious—there were four or five stores in the chain at the time, but there would be close to fifty by the time the chain folded—they had chosen a business they were passionate about. They did suspect, and correctly, that it was time for a chain of "literary" bookstores, but that veneer was more than simple marketing. They were serious about literature and its long tradition, and they expected the same attitude from their employees. Every few months, Ken and Kelly would come down from the central office to give new employees a little seminar on the history of the book and publishing and bookstores. They wanted to educate us in more than making change, balancing a register drawer, sweeping, and knowing which titles were climbing the best-seller list.

One Saturday Ken and Kelly took me into the back corner of the coffee bar with a stack of books and gave me a history lesson. First, they told me about the book itself. The right page was the recto, the left the verso. The pages of a hardcover were bound in groups called signatures; the pages of a paperback were cut flush and glued to the spine in a process called perfect-binding. Gutter, colophon, deckled; the words and terms spilled out. Then they led me through the progress of the book's development, from clay tablets incised with styli to papyrus scrolls, to hand-copied codices, to Gutenberg's movable type, all the way to mass-market paperbacks.

When Ken and Kelly recounted the history of publishing and bookselling, they told me that I had to keep in mind that the business had always been a cooperative one, guild-like, communal. Upstart Crow had attached ". . . & Company" to its name because booksellers and writers and publishers had been, for much of the history of the business, one and the same. And they had often worked in companies, groups of skilled merchants gathered under one sign. When we left Crow, Greta and I went to Printers Inc. Bookstore in Palo Alto, named so, without the possessive apostrophe, to imply that the store was a company of many. The Printers Inc. logo was the silhouette of a Gutenberg-era letterpress to indicate that we were more than merchants. It was a true Company that I worked for, one with a long, continuous history. "Listen," they kept saying that day. "Listen."

||||||

One of the earliest records of a bookseller is found in a hieroglyphic tomb inscription from the classical era of the Egyptian pharaohs, where it's noted that one undertaker has expanded his business by offering for sale to the grieving family his own edition of *The Book of the Dead.* This book (the ultimate "impulse" buy) would be placed with other funerary objects—clothes, toys, food, etc.—in the tomb with the deceased, where it would serve as a travel guide to the underworld. It's not a flattering beginning for the book trade, but it is fitting. In contrast to a modern caricature of the bookseller—in

cardigan with cat and tea—for centuries the bookseller
was regarded as a rogue, a hell-raiser, someone more
than capable of making a few quick bucks off the grief-
stricken, or of sowing the seeds of heresy and dissent.
From the beginning of the trade, the bookseller existed
independently, with little institutional or government
sanction or censor, and would act as the conduit for the
newest ideas and information of the day.

‖‖‖‖‖

The great library at Alexandria, which flourished for over
nine hundred years (c. 300 BCE to 642 CE), was a repository of "the books of all the peoples of the world." Under
the aegis of the Ptolemaic pharaohs (who were loyal to
their Greek installers), the librarians at Alexandria were
directed to confiscate, copy, and translate into Greek
every scrap of written matter that passed through the bustling port. All ships arriving in Alexandria were boarded
and searched for books, which were then taken to the
library and copied by its scribes; the copies were returned
to the ships, the originals remained in the library.

Historians estimate that the library held from 300,000
to 1,000,000 papyrus scrolls. These papyrus scrolls were
up to fifty feet long, but it took as many as ten to comprise a single book, and so the number of individual titles
in the library was probably between 50,000 and 100,000
at its height, around the same number you'd find in one
of today's book superstores. Still, the collection was un-
matched in the ancient world, impressive because all the

books were copied by hand, at a time when there were far fewer readers and writers. The library's collection was larger than any other library for nearly 1,800 years.

Alexandria was chosen as the library's site because of the city's political and economic importance. In an age of expanded empire and trading, Alexandria sat at the crossroads of Europe, Asia, and Africa. Situated on a narrow spit of land between an intertidal lake and the royal port at Pharos, the library was safely tucked inside the royal palace's fortified walls. The streets outside the library hosted a boisterous array of merchants, many of them booksellers. The word most often used to describe these booksellers was "unscrupulous."

The library's collection was intended for use by scholars, but booksellers often bribed the librarians to remove certain volumes, which were then copied by the bookseller and shipped to members of the Greek and Roman nobility in outlying regions. The hunger of the nobility for books seems to have been as much for status as for knowledge, leading one Stoic philosopher to ask, "Of what use are whole collections of books, when their owners barely find time in the course of their lives to read their titles?" The booksellers' questionable practices, however, saved many classical books from oblivion, for many of these pirated editions were the only copies to survive the destruction of virtually every scroll in the library.

The end of the library of Alexandria, after several centuries of sack and siege, came in 642 CE, when the armies of the Muslim caliph Omar conquered the city. Omar's liaison in Alexandria, the emir Ibn Amrou el-Ass, engaged one of the librarians, John Philoponus, in a debate that lasted almost two years, concerning the need to protect the vast collection. John Philoponus argued that these texts, predating the Prophet's arrival on earth, were not those of the infidel, but contained knowledge of God's word that the Muslims so assiduously studied. Amrou Ibn el-Ass conceded the importance of books to Arabic and Muslim culture and knew that many of the library's scrolls were Arabic in origin. Ibn el-Ass was swayed by the librarian's argument, and by the beauty and bounty of the library, but the fundamentalist caliph Omar was not; he remained convinced that the only book the world needed was *The Koran.* Omar ordered the library's books distributed to Alexandria's bathhouses, where they were burned to heat the waters. It took six months to burn them all.

How many books have been sacrificed to the fires of those who insisted on the need for only the one book: *The Koran, The Bible, Mein Kampf, The Communist Manifesto,* Mao's *The Little Red Book?* Too many, that's certain, but it's also certain that the tide of books cannot be stopped by fire.

||||||

The English word profane, which can mean common or secular or impious, comes from the Latin *profanus,* meaning "outside the temple walls." It is here, outside Alexandria's walls, that we find the first true booksellers, a pattern repeated in other countries. In medieval Europe, markets were often set up outside the walls of cathedrals; one such doorway, under the northern porch of Rouen Cathedral, is still called "le Portail des Libraries," the bookseller's gate.

The bookseller is profane in the figurative sense, too. By the time the Alexandrine marketplace appears, the selection of books available to any customer with enough cash has changed considerably from the one-stop shopping of the Egyptian undertaker. In an age of expanded trade, commensurate with a sharp rise in literacy—or is it vice versa?—the bookseller begins to offer books that had before been available only to the most powerful. Books, so rare until this time, had been dedicated to political and religious uses; the struggle to liberate books and their ideas from the hands of an elite will be a continual one, and booksellers play an important role in that liberation.

It was the power of the word that mattered, along with the ability to read. A few modern words reflect the notion that knowledge, literate knowledge, is a form of magic. Our word grammar, for instance, shares the same root as glamour; both derive from an early word that means magic. We call people witches because, or so we believe etymologically, they have their wits about them, they are learned. As more citizens of the Alexandrine empire became readers rather than listeners, they demanded a broader range of printed matter. The booksellers of Alexandria were providing more than guide books to the netherworld. There were romances and medical cures and ribald poems, scientific and philosophical tracts, prayerbooks, a selection as varied as today's: all the best and all the rest. The bookseller had become a bookstore.

||||||

The marketplace has existed since there has been a crossroads at which to display one's wares, a central plaza to occupy, or a city wall to park outside of. It continues today in many forms, from flea market to shopping mall. The market of early Alexandria would have been a vibrant one; this was the Greek age of empire, and the market brought together people and products that had never before crossed—foods and spices, textiles and tools. But beyond commerce, the Alexandrian crossroads also exchanged knowledge. As in other eras, when exploration and trade brought far corners of the world closer together—the Age of Exploration, the Age of Enlightenment, the Age of Rail, etc.—there was a sharp rise in literacy. The ability to read was needed to keep up with the new technologies and business practices. And mandatory reading is always followed by elective reading. The more readers, the more books needed; more books, more bookstores.

At Alexandria there would have been three distinct types of bookstores: the stall, a movable selection of books displayed on the ground or on a wheeled cart; the shop, a permanent structure either built into an arcade or freestanding; and the hawker, an itinerant bookseller, carrying his wares on his back from town to town.

|||||||

The bookstore begins as a simple stall, an area of earth claimed, momentarily, as retail space. In the earliest visual depictions—in classical Rome, in China and Japan, medieval Europe, and the Arabic countries—the bookseller is seated on the ground at a fair or market, his wares spread on a rug or displayed on a cart. The items for sale might include medicinal handbooks, various calendars and almanacs, erotica, primers for teaching children to read, and the ever-popular religious tracts.

I still find these stalls today. In my neighborhood, outside of a Laundromat and in front of the streetcar stop, every other Saturday or so, there's an old rug thrown on the sidewalk, and carefully placed on the rug are rows of hardcover and paperback mysteries. The purveyor of these goods is a regular guy with a good job, but he's a voracious reader, and he likes to spend Saturdays out on the sidewalk, reading in his deck chair and gathering a few coins—$1.00 for hardcovers, $.50 for paperbacks—which he undoubtedly spends on more books. I see these impromptu stalls all around the city, as they've been arranged in cites for thousands of years. Here's a well-trafficked spot, I've got some books—voilà, a bookstore. Garage sales, flea markets, sidewalk vendors.

I'm not much of a mystery reader, out of temperament more than anything else, but I still stop whenever

I come across this guy and his rug and his brightly colored police procedurals, manor-house mysteries, and psychological thrillers. They're not stolen; I can tell by the thumbed covers and cracked spines. It's the sudden bloom of it, I think, that stops me, this eruption from the sidewalk, like a gigantic, alien book-bearing vine. No, more like an underground spring that's suddenly been tapped, and here, this bright pool of books. And so I stop, as I must, just in case. And others do, too. By the end of the afternoon, practically all the books are gone.

IIIIII

As readers and books began to multiply, the market stall proved incapable of handling the trade. Bigger bookstores were needed, and most importantly, cheaper and faster printing methods had to be devised.

Until the sixth century CE in China, when block printing was invented, and the late fifteenth century CE in Europe, with the advent of Gutenberg's movable type, every copy of every book in the world was created by hand. At the book stall, most of the volumes would have been copied by the bookseller himself, and may even have been composed by him. Booksellers would also buy books from other merchants and copy them, make deals with those less-than-trustworthy librarians and scholars, or take on original manuscripts from ever-eager authors. During the early centuries of bookselling, the bookseller's greatest asset was a beautiful calligraphic hand; the best scribes demanded markedly higher prices.

In the Alexandrian market, the books would be written on papyrus, a reedy Nile plant made into a writing surface by cutting the plant's stem into narrow strips, which were then beaten to an airy thinness, dried in the sun, and pasted together into sheets. These sheets were glued to one another in long scrolls, which were stored in cedar oil in earthenware jars to prevent vermin and rot.

The papyrus scroll had two great disadvantages, however. If you wanted to leap ahead or backward in a scroll, you had to scroll and scroll. And while supple and plentiful, papyrus was also vulnerable to the elements and deteriorated quickly.

But it was cultural and economic jealousy that determined the shift from papyrus. The librarians at Alexandria knew that the rulers of Pergamum, in Asia Minor, were amassing a rival library; this rivalry created a keen competition between the two countries. In the rush to provide books for the new library, booksellers made thousands upon thousands of books, thus creating a great demand for papyrus. In the fourth century CE, to keep their advantage, Egyptians forbid the export of papyrus. To make up for the lack of papyrus, the librarians and booksellers of Pergamum used sheepskin or goatskin to create a new writing surface called parchment, which, in Latin means "of Pergamum." Although animal hides had long been used in writing and would continue to be used in the yet un-Europeanized Americas, parchment showed immediate advantages. After soaking in water, sheepskins were covered with lime to loosen the hairs, and the skins were scraped clean, stretched, and dried.

It might take twenty skins to make a small book, but you could eat the leftovers. And yes, that's why a diploma is called a sheepskin.

The real advantages to parchment, though, were that it lasted longer, and it was thin enough and sturdy enough to fold. It was parchment's pliability that made the transition from scroll to codex feasible. The codex is the modern book, comprised of pages attached to a book's spine that open along the axis of that spine. The origin of the codex lies in Roman accountants' ledgers, wax tablets joined at the edges by hoops. Because parchment could be folded, pages could be sewn together at the fold, into what we call signatures, and these signatures could be sewn into a spine, and placed inside a cover if necessary. The advantage of the codex is obvious, you're holding one in your hand right now: you can turn to any page instantly, there's no rewind. Parchment and the codex quickly gained favor with readers and booksellers, and the papyrus scroll became a relic.

Words have been written on everything. Some of the earliest extant writings, usually tax levies or other legal matters, are found on Mesopotamian clay tablets circa 3,000 BCE. These records were inscribed into wet clay that was then fire-hardened. The advantage to tablets is that fire poses no threat, but they are rather unwieldy. In India, early books were written on palm leaves; in China and Japan, pages were also made of silk, bamboo, and tree bark.

||||||

The Chinese invented paper. Legend has it that, in the first century CE, a court eunuch, Ts'ai Lun, saw odd bits of bark and detritus floating on the surface of a pond, and using a mesh screen, skimmed the pond, coating the screen with a pulpy surface that dried to become the first piece of paper. Documentary evidence suggests, however, that the Chinese were using paper at least two centuries before this. Legends aside, it is clear that Ts'ai Lun did perfect the papermaking process, for which contribution he was made a nobleman. Early Chinese books would be made of paper in a scroll form or folded in accordion-style pages.

Papermaking spread throughout Asia, and by the ninth century CE, had found its way into Arabic countries, and from there slowly to Europe. In Europe, paper was not commonly used until the sixteenth century, when the printing press and another spike in literacy threatened the livelihood of shepherds throughout the continent. Until this time, documents written on paper rather than parchment were not considered legally binding.

Paper was much cheaper than parchment or silk, more durable than papyrus or palm leaf, and lighter and less bulky than any of the materials used before. In the codex form, much more easily shipped and stored than the scroll, and with lightweight, thinner paper, books could contain more text, and more books could be made. And as always, more books, more readers, more booksellers.

|||||||

Nearly all booksellers carried a kit that contained the basic tools of his trade, an inkwell and styli. Most booksellers were also scribes for hire, a practice that continued in the bookstore into the nineteenth century. Virtually every bookstore was also a scriptorium, where those without the skill (that is, most everybody) could employ the scribe for their writing needs, whether it be legal or business documents, letters of news and longing to far-flung families or friends, or the seductively powerful love letter often composed by the scribe himself. If you were able to write, but unable to afford the materials in bulk, you could also rent and purchase time and supplies at the scriptorium, much the way some use Internet cafés today. The scriptorium, an integral part of the bookstore from its inception, probably helped establish, the leisurely pace of the bookstore. Take a seat and write a letter.

Many book stalls, and later, more established shops, offered reading privileges at a small cost, so that one might read a book without owning it. Reading rooms have always been an important aspect of the bookstore and have played an important role in the spread of knowledge during those times when the literacy rate had climbed but books were still too expensive to purchase. This tradition, which survived into the twentieth century as the lending library, has almost completely disappeared from the bookstore. For a small membership fee, patrons were enrolled in the library and could then check out books for small daily charges. Because bookstores have always been quicker to obtain new titles than libraries, readers could get their hands on them as soon as possible. Lending libraries were quite popular in the United States until the end of the WWII, when postwar prosperity and a new consumer culture made us all into great buyers rather than borrowers.

The stall where one might stop to buy a scroll, commission a love letter, or catch up on the most current use of leeches, could be exquisitely simple: one bookseller with pen, ink, paper, and a handful of attractively priced books spread on a carpet. Or it might be a cart on wheels, which could be moved from market to market, city to city, with shutters that locked at night. When business became steady enough, some of these carts found permanent homes, with a counter built into an arcade's overhang or church porch, eventually with the addition of sturdy walls on the side and back. The change to permanence created an enclosed area we would recognize as a shop. Perhaps the bookseller became prosperous enough to hire an assistant or two. It is from the simple market stall that the bookstore, a space to be entered and examined, evolves.

Bibliopolis, the City of Books

After four happy years at Upstart Crow, the time had come for me to move on, and in 1980, I went to work at Printers Inc., a large independent bookstore in Palo Alto. It was only twenty minutes north of Upstart Crow, but located on the edge of the Stanford campus, it was a world away in many respects. Greta and I went to Printers together, both of us frustrated with the growing corporate climate at Upstart Crow. We'd visited Printers on a few occasions and were impressed with its size, its comprehensive selection, and the vitality of the sales floor. On first glance, it seemed a bigger, more successful Upstart Crow, but we soon discovered that it was much more. Printers Inc., it turned out, was the center of a thriving community of writers, scientists, entrepreneurs, academics, and serious readers of all interests. Printers Inc. was a truly cosmopolitan bookstore.

|||||||

Before the end of the fifth century CE, when Christianity and its censors began to push Europe into the Dark Ages, Rome was the capital of an empire and a thriving literary cosmopolis, a haven for books, writers, and readers. At the time the literacy rate in Rome was higher than anywhere else in the world; public libraries were plentiful and open to all who could read; literary competitions were impassioned, frequent, and highly respected.

Newspapers were posted in public gathering places for all citizens to read, and the ensuing discussions and debates often tied up foot traffic. Personal scribes of the wealthy often copied these newspapers so that their patrons might read them, or better yet, have them read aloud at their leisure. The scores of daily newspapers in Rome were not unlike modern ones in their content—births and deaths, economic trends, natural disasters, political scandals, military exploits, and yes, even celebrity divorces.

In this atmosphere, the bookstore became a true trade, as vital to the city's makeup as any of its other rivers. In Classical Rome bookstores were abundant, fiercely competitive with one another, and could depend on an established distribution system as wide as the empire itself. Ovid, in exile near the Black Sea, recorded his relief upon finding copies of his work there, thousands of miles from his beloved city. Because Rome was far from the bathhouses of Alexandria and its attendant fires, and because its literature was not primarily confined to a single repository, i.e., the Great Library, more Roman than Greek writings survived the first millennium CE.

Although more established than its Mediterranean predecessors, the Roman book trade was still considered by most a somewhat disreputable profession. In the first century BCE, the lyric poet and satirist Horace in his *Ars Poetica* warned other writers to be leery of the up-start booksellers Sosii, the brothers Sosus who published many of his works. Sosii, he alleged, were less than hon-est in the number of copies they claimed to have sold, and he accused them of permitting pirated editions of his work to circulate. In other poetical works, however, Horace pays homage to Sosii for bringing fame to him and glory to Rome. How else would his works see the light of day, he asked, much less travel to the far ends of the Roman world?

In his poetry, no matter the ambiguity of his feelings for his booksellers, Horace is a savvy enough publicist to include directions to their stores. In his epistles he writes,

> Book of mine, I know why you look with longing
> To the gates of Janus and Vortumnus.
> You are impatient to arrive in the market,
>   dressed up
> In your new finery on the shelves of the brothers
>   Sosii.

The statue of Vortumnus, one of the mercantile gods, stood just outside the bookstore district; the temple of Janus stood near the entrance to the Forum, where mer-chants sold their various wares. The brothers Sosii op-erated one of the first bookstore chains, and you could purchase the newest volume of Horace at either of their convenient locations.

As the trade became more established, booksellers became publishers, in a modern understanding of the word, selecting what new works were to be published, taking on both risk and profit, and entering into legally binding (though still somewhat suspect) contracts with living authors. The bookseller as publisher is one of the longest threads in the trade's history, remaining unchanged until the industrial revolution of the nineteenth century.

To meet the demands of this burgeoning trade, more scribes were needed, and in Rome at this time, slave labor was plentiful. The wealthiest Roman households had long maintained private, often lavish libraries, and their household staff of maids, cooks, and gardeners would have included a reader/scribe. For many slaves, aside from the obvious luxury of being a scribe (as opposed to being a salt miner), the opportunity to learn to read and write was often the beginning of a road toward freedom.

One Titus Pomponius Atticus, in the first century BCE, expanded his shop and its services by bringing in a staff of slave-copyists to reproduce, on demand, the day's most popular books. His staff of copyists could duplicate an entire long book in one day, and quite cheaply. Through Atticus's shop one could purchase the first book of Martial's *Epigrams,* in a fancy edition, for five dinari, something less than ten of our dollars. A cheaper edition of the same book could be had for ten sestertii, about three dollars.

To accommodate the tide of new titles and the workers

who produced them, the shape of the bookstore began to change. No longer a mere façade—a rug or a stall—the bookstore deepened so that it could hold and display the rapidly increasing stock of books and provide backroom space for scribes and their supplies. The front counter, adapted from the cart and stall, would have remained, as it does today, the meeting place between customer and proprietor. On the counter, the newest books would be displayed. Behind the counter, and on the other walls in the front of the shop, boxlike shelves divided by smaller x-shaped shelves, would hold the stock of ready-to-read scrolls, with a small title tag attached to each. Scriptorium services would have also been available. And like the modern bookstore, author readings would have been a part of the scene; in the Forum, authors, both published and not, gathered in front of bookstores to recite their work in the hopes of finding an audience.

The evolution of the bookstore in Classical Rome is a watershed in the trade, albeit a five-hundred-year watershed. The shape of the Roman store, the deep shoe box with its seductive façade, still prevails today. In this era we also find that the notion of the bookstore as a place where many classes of citizens can buy inexpensive books becomes deeply imbedded in European culture. Books, once the sole property of priests and scholars, were common traffic now, secular and privately held.

IIIIII

When I stepped into Printers Inc., my first thought was a simple one. Printers was *shaped* like a bookstore, at least an idealized one. One narrow end of the shoe box opened onto the street, and the long, high sides of the store, lined with crammed shelves, seemed to pull the reader down their long avenues. In the vast middle of the store, display tables heaped with stacks of new titles competed with blocks of freestanding shelves for a customer's attention. The perspectives were clean and sharp, simple: a bookstore.

Upstart Crow, settled into a shopping mall whose spaces were designed to be flexible enough for any prospective merchant, was a jumble of small niches and demi-rooms under a low roof, a suburban sprawl of a store. Printers Inc., nearly four times the square footage of Crow, and with an eighteen-foot ceiling, was a Manhattan of a store, stately and massive.

The shoe box is a good shape for nearly any retailer. Its narrow entrance provides more storefronts on a shopping block, which is conducive to the realtor gaining more clients because the merchant can seduce more customers: more people with less space. On the way to one shop, the customer stops to gaze at another's well-appointed window display, is intrigued by an item there, opens the door of the shop, and voilà, a raft of merchandise that seemed impossible from outside.

Nor is the shoe box the only shape for bookstores. A bookstore can, and will, be crowded into the most ragged of spaces, a constant battle between rising rents and lower profits, and some of the world's great bookstores—Shakespeare and Co. in Paris and City Lights in San

Francisco are two that spring to mind—occupy spaces that twist and turn like mazes out of Wonderland, warrens and tunnels and tiny, odd-shaped rooms. Today's superstores occupy flat, cake-box, mall spaces whose floor plans are often identical to every other branch in the chain.

But the physical nature of books makes the shoe box a perfect fit. Of somewhat varying sizes, books are the same basic shape, slim rectangular blocks that can be easily stood one next to the other, two flat surfaces pushed together, each balanced at a ninety-degree angle to another flat surface: hence, shelves of books. Imagine how much more difficult to line up a shelf of cantaloupes. The shelving of books is made simpler by the firm but flexible nature of the paper and boards, and by the simple fact that books are their own packaging. It's no problem to slide one book out from between two others and return that book to the same spot on the shelf, as opposed to sliding one sweater out from a stack of sweaters.

If you can shelve something simply and securely, you can shelve it high up, and when you have 50,000 different kinds of fruit, no two of the same species even, a high shelf expands the space you're paying for: more books for less rent. Library ladders, as common to the bookstore as the library, make high shelves possible, and because of their uniform shape, books can be carried up and down ladders with relative ease and safety.

The high walls of the bookstore create a sense of intimacy. The colorful, packed shelves shorten and draw in the spaces much in the same way evening brings far hills closer. No one ever expects minimalist decor in a bookstore, no frigid tundra of tastefulness.

One thing is certain in the aesthetics of bookstore design: if there's too much space, there's not enough books, and pretty soon, customers will stop coming, and so the decline begins. Customers are seduced into a bookstore because it seems to thrive; we want to see lots of books. We are much more likely to be drawn to a messy bookstore than a neat one because the mess signifies vitality. We are not drawn to a bookstore because of tasteful, Finnish shelves in gunmetal gray mesh, each one displaying three carefully chosen, color-coordinated covers. Clutter—orderly clutter, if possible—is what we expect. Like a city. It's not quite a city unless there's more than enough.

The high walls and the taller freestanding shelves in a store create narrow aisles, deep canyons forming the streets of this city. These shelves are mostly given over to the backlist—the compressed, neatly alphabetized sections of books that were published prior to this season's new titles. These steep avenues of shelves are the city's working neighborhoods, where you stop to pick up that Hemingway you've been meaning to reread for years, the tax guide you'll be needing, your favorite kid's book for your favorite kid. Here in these pleasantly crowded streets you can stop and hide for a while, picking out this small corner of shelf, resting one elbow on it while you pore over a Joan Didion essay on the myth of California, or pulling up a stepstool for a minute with an eye-popping book of photos on the Day of the Dead celebration.

If the shelves are the skyscrapers that form the city's skyline, then a bookstore's display tables, flat and low, are the open parks and courtyards, where everything slows down a bit. Here you're supposed to take in what you've not seen yet, those books that can tempt you with a mere glance of their covers. No hurry; you could spend all day here. Like any great city, there's a mood for everyone, and like any great city, there's a surprise at every turn.

‖‖‖‖‖

Just inside the front doors to Printers Inc. was an antique letterpress, the store's logo and inspiration, one right out of the Gutenberg revolution and a symbol of the bookstore for hundreds of years. The letterpress was not mere decoration at Printers; it was a goal, a statement of the store's intention, and to make this intention more than a nice bookmark design, the owners set out to build a staff of the area's most experienced and dedicated booksellers. The store's founding owners— Jeffrey Shurtleff, Annie Leathers, Kate Abbe, Susan MacDonald, and Gerry Masteller—had all worked at Kepler's Books in nearby Menlo Park, which was one of the first, great paperback stores in the country, and among other distinctions, home to a vital antiwar movement in the 1960s. The first step in creating the Printers staff was to encourage the defection of as many Kepler's employees as possible.

After Printers opened in 1978, the owners began to aggressively recruit booksellers from other stores as well. The chief headhunter was Jeffrey Shurtleff, a laugh-out-loud, buzzing wire of a person who could light up any room with his smile. Jeffrey would drive around the Bay Area, from bookstore to bookstore, striking up friendly conversations with those of us who worked the front counters. The owners of Printers knew that a lot of us retail-slaves were enthusiastic about our roles as booksellers, and whether we worked for B. Dalton or Waldenbooks or Crow, were probably more than a little frustrated with our current positions and would be thrilled to find ourselves a new home in a more ambitious bookstore. Especially if we were asked. By the time Greta and I met Jeffrey, he'd already stolen one of our best employees, David Hodnett. By this time, Greta was managing, I was her assistant, and we thought of Crow as "our" store; we were dismayed, but understood when David took up their offer, earning more money and more responsibilities. Through David, Greta and I knew a great deal about Printers already, and the day that Jeffrey sauntered in, the three of us ended up chatting about bookstores and how impossible it was to make them work, the usual bookstore chat. He made us an offer to join the Printers staff, and we set up a meeting with the other owners.

Greta and I were easily seduced. First, there was the money. Printers felt, reasonably, that if they wanted a decent staff, they needed to offer decent compensation. Greta and I were offered wages one-third again higher than Crow's, and over the next few years Printers employees who worked half-time and more received free, extensive health benefits. The owners also established a profit-sharing plan that really worked (in four years of the plan I accrued nearly a full year's salary). Given that I had once threatened to quit Crow to secure a 10 cents-an-hour raise (a whopping $16.00 a month), it didn't take long for Greta and me to decide.

But it wasn't only the money; it never is with bookstore folk because the money's never *that* good. What Jeffrey described for Greta and me during that first chat, and what Kate, Susan, and Gerry reinforced during our long interview at Printers, was an opportunity to help build a great bookstore, a world-class bookstore. What book geek could pass on that?

Even before we got inside the store, when Greta and I arrived for our first meeting, we sensed that there was something different about Printers. Along the top of the high glass walls that formed the façade of the store, spelled out in not very elegant white stick-on letters was a repeated border of words "Books, Bücher, Livres, Libros." Inside we found sections of foreign-language titles to back the boast. We also found 1,200 magazines from around the world; a Poetry section larger than Crow's Fiction section; a Fiction section almost larger than Crow's entire stock; individual sections of Asian, Russian, and Middle Eastern histories, each one larger than Crow's History section, and American and European History sections that far outstripped the few shelves at Crow dedicated to these topics. Their Psychology section went far beyond *Looking Out for Number One,* and the Business section quite a bit was more sophisticated than *The Power of Positive Thinking.* There were long sections of specialized Chemistry, Biology, Mathematics, and Astronomy texts, most of them academic monographs and indecipherable to the common reader; and significantly, a section of technical computer-programming manuals at a time when few people owned computers.

All of this, and more, crammed into the city of books and laid out on the sunny display tables. It was pretty amazing. Greta and I had been to great bookstores together—the Bay Area, then and now, was chock-a-block with them—but what most swayed us about Printers? We'd been asked to help build this city of books.

‖‖‖‖‖

Palo Alto is no Manhattan. It's a leafy, manicured, affluent suburb devoted, or so it seems, to bike riding, jogging, tennis, and golf. It has none of the hustle and crush of a big city, and perhaps because of its seeming sleepiness, it may prove to be a better example of how a bookstore can create and galvanize a literary community. Any fool with enough cash can open a bookstore in Paris's Left Bank or on Bleecker Street in the Village (don't get me wrong, not any fool can make it work), but to open a world-class store in a neglected shopping street well south of Palo Alto's plush main drag takes some special, and lucky, fools.

310 California Avenue had much to recommend it as the location for a new bookstore. It was one mile from the Stanford University campus, only a few miles from the fledgling companies that would become Silicon Valley giants, and the rent was incredibly cheap. The latter cannot be overlooked. Location may be everything in retail, but part of the location equation is rent; with the low profit margin on books, a rent that's too high can forecast disaster.

California Avenue was a short three blocks of faded shopping that seemed to have stalled in the late 1950s. The vast space that Printers came to occupy had once been a butcher's, a grand butcher shop with knee-crushing cement floors. The street had one dive bar and one fern bar, a lonely single-screen theater, a not-very-good Chinese restaurant, a wheat-grass and tofu health store, and several knickknackeries. California Avenue, quiet during the day, was a ghost town at night. Until Printers opened its doors.

At the time, Palo Alto and neighboring Menlo Park were well stocked with good bookstores: Kepler's, Stacey's Business and Technical Books, Stanford's extensive campus bookstore, Shirley Cobb's carriage-trade hardcover store, and a number of used and antiquarian booksellers. The owners of Printers faced that age-old question, "Do we really need another bookstore?" and somehow convinced themselves, contrary to reason, that the answer was yes.

Like so many clever merchants before them, the owners of Printers stole all their best ideas. The trick was mixing the stolen ideas in a new way. Printers offered the complete selection of new books that Kepler's did, but more of them; they offered the business and technical titles that so many of Stacey's customers sought; they offered the extensive academic and special-order services that Stanford's campus store provided; they hosted readings two and three times a week by famous and yet-to-be-famous writers; they took their cue from the great newsstands of Berkeley and Cambridge; and they topped it all off with a coffee bar straight from the pages of Upstart Crow. One-stop shopping for the Stanford and Silicon Valley communities. Oh, we stayed open late, too, till midnight.

After only a few months in business, it was clear the store would be a success, and soon, it had revitalized the entire street. It became, in retail-speak, an anchor store, a destination. More restaurants were springing up, a nightclub for live music, upscale clothing and decor stores, copy shops, other cafés. The place was jumping. Tax revenues climbed. High school kids hung out till all hours. Parking was impossible. Street life.

For someone who'd come from the quietest of suburbs, and who'd tasted only a sliver of cosmopolitan life at Crow, I found the scene at Printers a thriving one, urgent. In San Jose, the bohemian crowd at Crow was an oddity, a rarity. At Printers the cultural scene that exploded in and around it was not an anomaly. It was everyday. The life of the village that grew up around Printers was based on books and the primacy of them in one's life, not on books as one more shopping outlet. If only for three short blocks, the center of this city was the bookstore.

‖‖‖‖

There was a simple imperative at Printers: the store had to stock everything. A directive the store was successful enough to support, but one that required a large staff to implement. As part of a chain, Upstart Crow offered little leeway in what the individual store could order; the bulk of the ordering was done at the central office, using graphs and charts that employed rational shelf-inch measurements (i.e., the A-B shelf of Fiction could only be 44-inches long and no longer). Greta and I did find a way around these strictures. We took to inventing special-order customers—Lumchuck Hickle was one of my favorites, and the much too obvious Marcel Duchamp. These imaginary customers frequently purchased three copies of the newest literary essays or five copies of the year's best avant-garde drama. No one at the central office ever remarked on what gangbuster business we were doing in multiple-copy special orders.

But Printers was an independent store—in all the best applications of that word—and the owners gave us more than free rein, they turned us loose. With stacks of publisher catalogues in one hand, and piles of green and white inventory cards in the other, we set out into the stacks to keep track of every single book that was sold, and to re-order it, and to discover what those sales might tell us about the titles we did not yet stock. When I wasn't behind the register, I was out in the city of books, endeavoring to make it a more crowded city. All those years we were, in the parlance, working the floor. It's a retail phrase I've always loved, "Yeah, I'm on the floor." Good place to be.

One of the less-publicized compensations of working in a bookstore, one that has always given me pleasure and reward, is the nature of the workspace itself, from behind the register to the back room, and especially the sales floor, which in any good bookstore is where most of the work gets done, hands-on. The nature of the bookstore workspace is one of freedom and flexibility, the sense of being in the public arena while doing private tasks, the sense of involvement with the day and the strangers who wander through it. This is the public square, an extension of the street, the marketplace. And physically, sensually, working the floor offers more air to breathe than cubicle or office life, a keener sense of the day's changing light, the shape and curve of the seasons. Working the floor is working *in* the world, being a part of it, rather than stowed away from it.

I'd move from section to section, with stacks of inventory cards, to check the date and frequency of sales. I'd pull books from the shelves to see whether they should be returned or not, and more often than not, I'd pull a book from its shelf simply to find out more about it. All of this with the sun streaming in, or whatever the world had in store that day.

Most of my time at Printers was spent without a computer-inventory system, which we only installed in 1985. Our one book/one card inventory system was labor intensive, tedious, and ultimately enlightening. It was not possible with this system—each book had a card in it, green for hardcover, white for paperback, which was removed at the register when it was sold—to sit in front of a computer screen all day and read lists of titles and their associated numbers. We had to go to the shelves, which meant we had to touch the books, which meant we had the opportunity to know more about them. What I've learned about a good many things of the world, both trivial and profound, often started with the back of a book, a sentence read there that led to another book that led to even more books. A bookseller's mind tends to get cluttered with these tiny strokes of information—Fibonacci numbers, wildfowl-migration patterns, Abyssinian folktales, violin varnishes of the sixteenth- and seventeenth-century Italian masters—but it's a pleasurable enough addiction. The same might be said of Internet research, one blip leading to another, but with one important difference. In the bookstore, the book is there at hand, ready for immediate consumption.

Perhaps what was most invigorating about the inventory system at Printers, and about working the floor in general in any bookstore, computer system or not, is that the work remains physical in nature. With a computer-inventory system a bookseller can sit in front of a computer screen all day and all night, but sooner or later he must get off his butt and put the books on the shelves.

When we weren't doing inventory, or should I say before we even started inventory, we had to shelve all the books, and at a high-volume store like Printers, the shelving on any given day would literally add up to thousands of pounds; during the Christmas rush, this could double or triple, two or three tons of books, all to be shelved one at time, in miles of aisles. You load up a cart full of books, broken down by section, and go off onto the floor as fast as you can, but stopping when you need to because there's something about the title of this Argentinean novel that's too intriguing to pass up. And then back to the shelving.

And it's a Friday night, so it's really busy, and you have to maneuver the cart around a family eating slabs of chocolate cake and reading B. Kliban cartoons together in the Biography section. You're trying to get through this cart of books because the weekend should be busy, bonkers in fact, the holidays are looming, but every time you finish with one customer, there's another. Hey, can you help me find, and so you traipse off to Cookbooks to help locate a recipe for St. Louis BBQ ribs, and you find it, but then there's somebody there who needs help finding a gift for a twelve-year-old boy (no gift is harder to choose), and in the middle of that the phone's ringing off the hook, and you answer those calls as you can, and still you're trying to help this one guy with some Computer books. And you stop and look around, and it's exhilarating. The register line is long, and every once in a while Susan, who's working there, has to buzz for help to get through all the customers, although sometimes she's just buzzing because she knows David will join her there, and this will give them an excuse to hang out together; they're falling in love on store time, and they think that no one knows. The store is jammed, the coffee bar is overloaded, and no one here is without a book. You recognize the famous writer (the not-yet-famous one is writing at a table in the coffee bar) and the beautiful folk singer, and the guy, rumor has it, who's invented something called Virtual Reality.

Everybody wants something, no, they need it, the title of a poem or a series of equations used in the prediction of cellular growth in single-cell animals, and you can't believe how lucky you are to be working in this city of books.

On the Road

The book trade in Asia, notably in China and Japan, was widely established by the end of the first millennium CE; the earliest extant drawing of any bookseller is found in a Chinese painting circa ninth century CE. Although the Chinese experimented with movable type as early as the eleventh century, they did not fully adopt modern printing technologies until the nineteenth century.

In that early portrait, the proprietor of the shop stands behind the front counter, under a tiled roof, helping two female customers with their purchases. The women are standing on the market side of the counter. The bookseller has laid out several volumes for their approval, one hand raised as if in explanation. On the shelves directly behind him, stacks of new books await readers.

Other technological innovations created a type of bookseller that was unique to China, and which would only appear in Europe in a significant way after the Gutenberg revolution. Chinese booksellers had used paper since the first century, and in the sixth century they began to use block printing. These changes produced books and pamphlets that were far cheaper and much lighter than earlier books. A bookseller could now strap selected titles to his back and wander the countryside. It's in China that we find the first pictorial record of the hawker, the door-to-door bookseller.

In block printing, the text and illustration of an entire page is carved, backwards, into a piece of wood, which is then inked and pressed to paper. Block printing allowed the bookseller to print not only editions of extant works, but also books that might appeal to those readers outside literary, urban centers. Calendars and almanacs were needed by farmers, and every family could benefit from the latest medical information. As it has been since books were first written, ribald romances were as popular in first millennium China as anywhere else. The selection the early hawker sported was something akin to that of the wire racks that crowd grocery-store checkout stands—diets, horoscopes, cheesy novels.

These block prints were early paperbacks, bound accordion-style most often, or simply sewn into signatures, unencumbered by the wooden or leather covers then in vogue in Europe. An enterprising young peddler would stock up on these paperbacks, along with other items—medicines, decorative trinkets, toys, and religious charms—and hit the road, traveling from village to village, farm to farm. Chinese and Japanese hawkers carried wooden or bamboo shelves on their backs. Their shelves, often six feet or taller, were decorated with ribbons and flags, and other eye-catching devices. The hawkers themselves wore particularly garish clothes to attract attention.

European book hawkers, who became more common after the invention of the printing press when cheaper editions became available, also wore gaudy clothes, but instead of shelves on their backs, they preferred baskets slung across their bellies, which gave them an air of early-day Johnny Applebooks, sowing seeds of knowledge across the countryside. The selection of books and tracts the European hawkers offered would have been similar to that of Asian hawkers: books on religion, health, sex.

The tradition of the hawker thrived into the nineteenth century, especially in the United States where most of the population lived on farms and in small towns. Noah Webster, the great lexicographer and re-speller, hit the road himself, by carriage and by train, to sell his dictionaries and to promote his notion of a wholly American language and spelling system. During the nineteenth century, 90 percent of all books sold in the United States were purchased from traveling book agents. For thousands of years, around the world, this was how most readers outside the city walls obtained their books, by taking notice of the bright rags and flags of a stranger coming down the road.

In twentieth-century America, the book hawker continued his travels in the guise of the door-to-door encyclopedia or family-Bible salesman (at sixteen I went to an orientation for prospective door-to-door encyclopedia sellers and was relieved to discover you only had to carry one volume on your rounds; still, I declined the chance). But the creation of the parcel post system in the late 1800s and the concurrent rise of catalogue sales made the itinerant book hawker unnecessary, at least for house-to-house calls.

The itinerant book hawker has been reincarnated today as the publisher's sales representative, the commercial traveler who moves from city to city and bookstore to bookstore. The sales rep is the direct link between the publisher and the bookstore, and while all such work might easily be done by phone or mail (or fax or e-mail), the nature of the bookstore requires that the sales rep go on the road.

Wouldn't you know it, just when I thought it was time for me to get out of the bookstore, after six swell years at Printers Inc., I got a job as a publisher's sales rep, and spent my days, not in one bookstore, but traveling to three or four a day.

‖‖‖

While I was excited to move deeper into the publishing world, I was a alarmed at the idea of becoming a salesman. The bookseller was a merchant, a member of the community, a committed professional. To become a publisher's rep carried with it the danger, I believed, of my becoming a Salesman, a hand-shaking, fast-talking, "Hey, nice tie, how's the wife and kids, sure looking good, you working out?" sort of Salesman. An odd fear,

I knew; I'd known hundreds of sales reps, professionally and otherwise, at Printers, and few were ever like that, but still, we fear for ourselves what we'd never imagine for others. But I was proved wrong about the Salesman metamorphosis. Publishers sales reps rarely become Salesmen; they remain, in most ways, booksellers, still part of the family.

So I donned my suit and tie, got a new car, and hit the road. It only took me a few months to discover that the suit and tie weren't really necessary, and this was a relief. The bookstore provides a casual atmosphere. There are a few fashion dandies in the bookselling world, but the usual jeans and T-shirt uniform has a lot to do with the physical nature of the bookstore. Who wants to lug stacks of fifty-pound boxes in a suit and bow tie?

I even encountered resentment from some booksellers to the suit and tie. Russ Solomon, who started Tower Records and Books, made his opinion of suit-and-tie wearers quickly known. In the early days of the Tower, when Russ did the majority of the buying for both the record and bookstores, he would reach across his desk with a pair of scissors and snip off the tie of any sales rep who hadn't yet learned the lesson. On the wall behind him was a rainbow fan of expensive and cheap, tasteful, and gaudy ties, all stapled there. So the legend has it.

After my first summer as a sales rep, after receiving a lot of long, hard stares, and after a couple of 100-degree weeks in California's San Joaquin Valley, I hung up my suit and tie and went back to my bookselling uniform, that is, whatever was most comfy that day. There was an equality to this dress, a sense that we were all on the same side. In all my time as a bookseller and a rep, there was only one person who could dress beyond the station. Oliver Guilliland, bless his soul, was the Norton sales rep for decades, beloved by all, and he wore vintage suits, ties, and shoes. Oliver was a snappy dresser, no matter his profession. Oliver wasn't opting for the simplistic, business uniform of our times, the suit and tie that says "I'm a power guy." Oliver had style, rare in any world. We allowed him his suits because of his style, and we envied him just a little. But most of us stuck to casual, reps and booksellers, because we were in it together, and we were in the back room, employees only.

||||||

I use the word Salesman for both men and women because it captures something of the occupation's essence, a tone and definition, that salesperson simply doesn't. The emphasis is on Sales; you can sell anything when you're a Salesman, you are *in* Sales. When it comes to sales rep, the initial letters are lower case, and the emphasis is on rep, a representative or liaison, a go-between. You don't sell just anything when you're a rep; you sell books. Semantic of me, I know, but semantics often point to real divisions; nuances count.

Consider the term "cold call." A true Salesman has to make cold calls, must contact someone who has not asked to see him. In this way, the traditional book hawker is a true Salesman, knocking on doors unbidden, but still he is selling books, and when you care about books, this does make a difference. And it made a huge difference to me that publishers' sales reps did not have to make cold calls.

A sales rep has two or three seasons a year in which new books are published and must be sold—Spring, Fall, sometimes Winter—and for each of these seasons, the rep makes an appointment at the local bookstore, usually with the same buyer. It's a familiar endeavor, a first-name transaction, Hey, Gerry, it's Lewis, when can I see you? It's a sales call, but it's not cold.

The purpose of this call is more about representing than sales. A good sales rep knows each bookstore's trade and specialties, and so tailors the presentation to those titles in the publisher's list (or lists; some reps may show ten or twenty or a hundred catalogues from different publishers). The job of the sales rep is to teach the buyer about the new titles, so that the buyer can make calculated decisions as quickly as possible, saving more time to talk about other books.

Or talk about baseball or politics or where to have lunch that day—on the rep's expense account, of course. In the back room it's hard to maintain the professional demeanor required of most Salesmen. Bookstore back rooms are messy, cluttered, and intimate because they are shut off from the floor and the rest of the world.

When I was a sales rep I loved going to stores, seeing

what each had to offer, taking in the unique atmosphere, even finding myself stranded there, as I did one rainy day in Eureka on California's rainswept north coast, waiting for a tardy buyer and reading all of Richard Ford's *The Sportswriter* in front of the shop's fireplace. But what I loved most was hanging out in the back room.

‖‖‖‖‖

What distinguishes a bookstore's back room is the volume and the shape of its clutter. It will be a mess, that's for certain, boxes of books stacked and tilting precariously, order forms and catalogues covering every square inch of desk, boxes of stripped mass-market covers and the corresponding boxes of stripped mass-market books, old magazines, with their covers and without. And publishers' promotional items, posters and cardboard cutouts of Hillary Clinton, and buttons and keychains and bumper stickers, and decorative marketing folders and bound galleys of forthcoming books. The back room of the bookstore is surging sea of paper, the many varieties paper can hold. At Printers, our green and white inventory cards, bundled and loose, dotted the landscape, and if you opened the drawer of any desk, you found even more; at Crow the same was true with the paper inventory system there, small perforated tags stuck to the inside covers and removed at the point of sale, then gathered for inventory reports. But these days what mostly threatens to drown any open space are floods of computer printouts.

When Printers switched to a computerized inventory in 1985 (a watershed year in the computer conquering of the world, it seems now, when suddenly people had computers at home, and even the QuickieMart's register beeped and clanged), the purveyors of the IBID computer inventory system assured us that society would soon be paperless. Hooray, we said. Alas (a word that so often follows hooray), this prediction couldn't have been more wrong. The computer inventory system seems nothing but a perpetual printer, whose waves of black-dotted foam continue to roll, ceaselessly. And because it's a computer, with all the authority we've invested in that word and conceit, it's incumbent upon us to pay homage to the machine and its printouts. Computers have made inventory control faster and more effective—but only to a certain degree. How often have you heard this phrase from a well-meaning if overworked and underpaid retail employee, "Well, the computer says we don't have it." The computer can be wrong, and that book can be there on the shelf. Ninety-nine percent of the time, the computer and its printouts are correct enough, but that 1 percent is an important margin of error because it might be the book your customer absolutely has to have that day.

|||||

As the itinerant hawker must have enjoyed seeing other people's countries and lives and homes, so the sales rep inherits a voyeur's dream. Settled among the back room's sea of paper, in an uncomfortable chair, discussing books with the buyer, the sales rep gets to watch the lives of many booksellers played out. The arguments among the staff, the frequent parties, the happily lonely hours unpacking boxes of books, solitary lunches hunched over a new book. The bitching and yelling about customers; the hiring and firing. It's here where those love affairs begun on the sales floor are often consummated, often at night after the store's closed. The back room is a clutter and flux of lives, a near-family. I know there are affairs and friendships and near-families in other lines of work, but I return to simple shapes. There are no walls here, no cubicles, just a big room where everyone works together, and the sense that just outside the door, not empty hallways, but a bustling world of customers and other lives. The back room is not unlike the space where Roman scribes once sat copying their works onto papyrus and parchment (and undoubtedly bitching about their customers), and where today the bookseller sits poised with a pen over a computer printout.

‖‖‖

The work of being a sales rep is mostly in the talking. Here's a book, here's what it's about, how many can I put you down for? Depending on the book and the buyer, this can be a lot of fun. Or not. A certain monotony can set in; it all depends, in the end, on how much you like to talk, and your ability to repeat yourself without going crazy. But there were two pleasurable elements to sales repping I hadn't expected.

In traveling from bookstore to bookstore, and having scores of conversations each week with booksellers, bigger pictures began to form about how a specific book was selling—and not just one from the rep's own list, or the latest insipid best seller, but that surprise seller. The conversation would then expand to include not only that book but that subject or type of book, and what those sales might mean for the prospects of a small publisher. What I often learned from one book buyer would be echoed by many more, multiplied a hundred times and painted now on a larger canvas. The excitement in this larger conversation was, in part, in being the messenger, saying to one bookseller a hundred miles distant that another was having luck with this memoir about life in the circus, and then passing this info on to even more booksellers, and watching each have success with that title. It's a wonderful feeling of inclusiveness. Not that one person can be responsible for such successes—publishing's too big and complicated a web for such vanity—but it does matter that one rep can be a strand of the web, that even though publishing is a complicated, messy, and undoubtedly inefficient business, good books still find their way to the hands of readers.

But the greatest pleasure I found as a sales rep came through decidedly noncommercial and one-on-one transactions. Sales reps get to give away books. Comps, complimentary copies. Hey, let me comp you one of those. I carried a little pad with me where I wrote down the names of the books and where they should be sent. The choice of the books was limited to my own publisher, but that was always enough. It's a common practice—and a smart one.

Free books are the true great perk of being a bookseller, and when that free book arrives, the bookseller is more than likely to look fondly on it, and to know more about it, and so will probably sell more copies of it. This is the theory behind comps, and it does work in the real world.

Along with comps, booksellers also receive paperbound galleys of forthcoming titles—ARCs or Advance Reading Copies. The excitement of the ARC is obvious, one gets to read it before anyone else, and that excitement often promotes more handselling of a given title. Comp copies and ARCs are cheaper and more effective than print or other forms of advertisement, and they're direct, going to the people who actually work on a book's behalf—receiving, shelving, displaying, putting it in a paying customer's hands.

When the business of the sales call was over, I'd ask the buyer if she wanted any comps. The answer was always yes. Then I'd go around the back room and ask the other booksellers—the receiving clerk, the returns person, the children's buyer, the whole gang—and then I'd go out on the floor and ask the bookseller at the front desk, and anyone else who happened to be around. Free books for everybody! These free books would not increase my territory's overall sales in any explicit manner, or the bookstore's annual sales; many comps never get read, and a few end up back in the warehouse from whence they came. But that's not the point. The point is that it was a pleasure, for all involved, but for me particularly. I got to pass on to other readers books that I loved, books I felt were important. And all for free.

||||||

Being a rep on the road has its more traditional perks, too. Nice car, nice hotel rooms, nice restaurants, and the nice credit card to pick up all these expenses. It's a catered life, all on the house. A rep's license plate should read, Eat Free or Die. There's the freedom (and exhaustion and frustration) of driving all day, especially down those long stretches of road, the radio cranked up, the windows open, and in my territory, northern California, the beauty of the landscape—Mendocino to Monterey, and all spots between. The small towns, the friendly people, getting out of the city for a while, new vistas, like a vast butte of wildflowers rioted with purple and yellow one late spring outside of Chico.

For some, it's the perfect job, living in a hotel for a week at a time, traveling to different stores. There are reps who've built a life out of this transience, who've embraced it. And depending on the territory, the embrace might have to be huge. I knew a rep whose territory for several smaller publishers was the entire northwest corner of the Unite States, from Washington to Montana down through Oregon and Colorado, a great big square piece of land. He had no apartment or home, only a Jeep with a clothes rack and awesome frequent-flyer miles from a favorite hotel chain.

Perhaps because I'd grown up in bookstores, I had come to depend on that sense of place and community, and eventually I found the sales-rep life and its overall lack of place unsettling. I grew tired of the other people's places. One night, I found myself in a lovely hotel room, with my room-service meal, when I happened to channel-surf upon a bleak and grainy documentary from the early 1960s about door-to-door Bible salesmen in the rural southern United States. The motels these salesmen stayed in were cinder-block and had no room service at all, certainly no Jacuzzi, but still, I sensed the connection. Bleak and grainy, indeed. After seven years, it was time for me to come in off the road.

Out of Darkness

The Middle Ages were unkind to Europe's book-sellers. Many of the great humanistic and civic advances of the Greek and Roman empires were either eradicated or forced into hiding. The barbarians were always at the gate, it seemed, and so the gates were shut tight. The Christian empire sought to defend its slippery purchase on the good souls of Europe by exercising rigid controls over free thought and its public expression. The burgeoning literacy and the flourishing trade in books of pre-Christian Rome were not well suited to the Middle Ages. Henry Curwen, in his *History of Booksellers,* phrases it gracefully: "Men were too busy in giving and receiving blows, in oppressing and being oppressed, to have the slightest leisure for book-learning."

For nearly a thousand years, publishing in Europe was virtually confined to Bibles, church-sanctioned religious tracts, and those classic works—science and philosophy—only a privileged few could access. Most new books during these centuries were hand-copied by monks for their own studies and devotions. Some monastic orders also copied manuscripts to sell or barter. Books were so valuable during this time that they were customarily chained to desks or placed on shelves behind locked, iron grates.

The form and expense of the medieval book had as much to do with the shrinking tide of knowledge as with the church's censorship. Catholic theology decreed that glory was to be accorded to the holy things of this world; magnificent cathedrals strove to touch the heavens, the robes and miters of those anointed to the church were bedecked with gold and jewels. And so it followed that the books that held the true word incarnate had to be works of art. Their covers were adorned with gold leaf, ivory, and precious gems, and their pages illuminated with the most ornate and costly scripts and illustrations. The codex had long replaced the scroll as the most common form of written communication, but the book covers of the Middle Ages were heavy, wooden boards (most often beech wood, in German *buche,* hence our word *book*), sometimes covered in leather. The books themselves were oversized—mostly to deter theft—and altogether cumbersome. One scholar complained that an important reference work was so unwieldy it required two desks to support it. The veneration of the sacred word can be seen as a rather clever form of censorship. Books were neither cheap nor plentiful, and very difficult to steal.

The one major development in the book trade during the Middle Ages came with the appearance of the university in Europe in the first centuries of the second millennium, circa 1100–1400. The university, a concept imported from Arabic culture, was nothing more than a library in which students and teachers read and discussed books. The university was also the beginning of the end of the darkness of the Middle Ages, a long and difficult striving to a humanism that would not flower until the Renaissance. Because of the universities more books were needed, and because the books were being sold to students, they had to be cheaper and less elaborate than the illuminated masterworks of the monasteries.

To supply this demand, a new class of copyist proliferated, an expansion abetted by the introduction of paper into Europe (yet another innovation introduced by Arabic culture). As well as providing the writing services they had for centuries, European booksellers of this era sold paper goods and supplies to a growing population of students. Since most booksellers were housed in permanent stalls or shops, they were called *stationarii* (where we get our word for paper stationery). Especially in Paris, under the protection and guidance of the Sorbonne, the *stationarii* flourished; the descendants of the *stationarii* can be found in the green-painted, wooden stalls of the *bouquinistes* that crowd the banks of the Seine today.

The tie between the university and the book trade helped both institutions proliferate in Europe. But the next development in the book trade will be the one that catapults it, and all of Europe it seems, into the bright light of knowledge.

||||||

The histories tell us that Johannes Gutenberg invented his movable-type printing press in 1438 CE in Mainz, Germany. Gutenberg, a goldsmith, had been tinkering with movable type for a few years, fashioning individual letters that could be rearranged and reused in an inexpensive and infinite series of combinations. But it was more specifically the combination of this type in conjunction with a wine press that made modern printing feasible. It took Gutenberg years of experimenting before he printed his first Bible, the famous 42-line Gutenberg Bible of 1454. Like hand-copied books of the day, the Gutenberg Bible carried no title page and no publisher information.

As with any historical watershed, the invention of Gutenberg's printing press was not an isolated moment of insight. Europe was emerging from the suffocating religiosity of the Dark Ages; by the end of the fifteenth century, transoceanic exploration had begun, the Reformation was diluting the power of the Catholic church, and the Renaissance was in full swing. The ascendancy of the university, and yet another spike in the literacy rate, due in part to freer trade and improved economic conditions, added to the demand for books. Book makers all over Europe strove to find faster ways to meet this new demand.

Block printing, borrowed from China and Japan, had been used in Europe for at least a hundred years before the Gutenberg Bible, but it was an inexact printing method and could not compete aesthetically with illuminated manuscripts. In Europe block printing was used primarily for devotional prints of the saints, which one purchased at the end of a pilgrimage to gain indulgence for some of the lesser sins. Block printing was also used in the making of playing cards, a new and popular pastime, especially in Venice. It was still illegal to print such secular items, and most of this business was conducted on the far edge of the law, where many booksellers seem to have begun their careers. Entire books of block printing were created around this time, but they were contemporary with the Gutenberg Bible.

There are earlier printed books than Gutenberg's, several of them Dutch, most notably those of Laurens Janszoon Coster of Haarlem, but their quality was markedly inferior to Gutenberg's. The refinements Gutenberg brought to the printing process made it economically feasible.

Gutenberg's training as a jeweler inspired him to create the tools and casting methods for the thousands of pieces of type needed for any large print job. He adapted coin punches to typeface, striking the reverse impression of a letter into a softer metal, then filling this indentation, or matrix, with a molten mixture of lead, tin, and antimony, which hardened on contact and created a raised piece of type. These pieces would be arranged on a composing stick, which was fitted with other sticks into a printing form, creating a mirror-image page. The printing form was secured into the modified wine press, inked, and pressure applied until the page took the impression. The other crucial modifications that Gutenberg created in his workshop were a quick-drying ink and a refined paper that held crisp edges. Mechanized over the centuries but basically unaltered, Gutenberg's printing press was still in use until the introduction of various photographic printing methods in the early twentieth century.

By the time Columbus first stumbled on the Americas, the printing press was an established technology and could be found in almost every European city. By the end of the sixteenth century the printing press had spread across Asia as far as Japan, and into the Americas via Peru. Numbers best demonstrate the success of Gutenberg's invention. A printer could create in one day what it might take a single monk six months to accomplish. It's estimated that before the printing press, there were only 50,000 books in all of Europe; fifty years after Gutenberg's first Bible, there were more than 20 million.

Somebody had to sell these books. The European bookselling community established guilds and trade organizations, attempted to create an effective copyright system, and battled the censorship decrees of both church and state. The most popular book in the immediate post-Gutenberg centuries, hot on the heels of the Reformation, was any Bible in a language other than Latin, that is, a language someone could actually read; in sixteenth-century England there were over 300 different English-language versions of the Bible produced. The next most popular titles were children's ABCs and first primers. Europe was learning to read.

||||||

A customer of the early age of printing would have entered a bookstore similar to one today, yet with some distinct differences. From the fifteenth to the eighteenth centuries, books were stored horizontally on their shelves, rather than vertically, and the spines would have faced the backs of the shelves rather the customer. Most books would lack covers (title pages, however, were now included), be completely unbound, and stacked in loose quires (signatures of twenty-four pages). After choosing a book, the customer would then select the color and cost of binding that would most suit the volume and his library decor. Or one could choose to read the book as is, without covers, an early prototype of the paperback. After the eighteenth century, books were sold in their bindings, and shelved vertically and spine out, as they are today.

In the back room, instead of scribes, there would be a printing press and a binding machine, as well as a cache of wooden barrels, which were used to store and transport books from the Middle Ages until the end of the nineteenth century.

What most marked the shape of these bookstores was the front counter, a combination of a printer's desk—with all the minutiae required of that enterprise—and service counter. Here a bookseller could work on his next publishing project and still be ready to serve and charm his customers. And in all the illustrations of bookstore interiors from the Renaissance on, it's the counter that predominates, that narrow and cluttered

104 ≡ Lewis Buzbee

island of space that separates, and yet connects, bookseller and customer.

||||||

The front counter of today's bookstore is where the cash
register sits expectantly, and there's probably a phone
as well, along with a ragged jar of pens and pencils, a
stack of store bookmarks, and any number of impulse
items—book lamps, laminated maps and tip charts, audio
CDs, and miniature books of varying shape and silliness.
Behind the counter, and underneath it, there's a storm
of things and stuff: rolls of gift wrap, a ragged selection of books with customers' names rubber-banded
around them, a stereo and its attendant clutter, drawers
of forms and paper clips and spare keys, a message board
or log book for the edification and venting of employees,
magazines with stripped covers waiting to be recycled,
and a lost-and-found box filled with sunglasses, scarves,
umbrellas, scribbled-in notebooks, a shirt or a jacket, and
empty wallets. Pigeon- and cubby-holes. There was a time
when there were cigarettes in ashtrays, too.

But no matter how chaotic the front counter, there's
always a smooth, clean place to which the customer
can sidle and drop a stack of purchases, a focal point of
orderliness, a small path of clarity that allows for transaction. During the lulls of a business day, that open
space is just the spot for a bookseller to plant her elbows
and keep an eye on things.

The front counter is a command center much like the

deck of a ship, a surveillance roost against theft and mayhem, and a trading post. Like the bar in a saloon, it is also a barricade against and haven from the public, a seat of power and security. Ideally the bookseller is a messenger of the gods (for centuries the book trade's symbol was wing-footed Mercury delivering truth and art). A bookseller is, first and last, the custodian of a wonderful space, a groundskeeper concerned with the order and care and stock of that space. The bookseller both maintains and presents the space to the public, while at the same time protecting that space and its contents from the same public. Day-to-day bookselling is more about the physical world than the loftier realms. Retail—bookstores in particular—can be harder on your knees and back than on your mind.

The front counter offers a respite from the endless rounds of straightening, lifting, and toting, and if you're lucky, there's a tall stool to lighten the load. And whether the store's on Alcatraz Island, or in the Grand Tetons, or next to the San Francisco Opera, there's usually a front window, a vantage to the street-side of the store, where the world and weather pass by, the day traipsing through the curve of hours and falling gently into evening and night. From this turning world comes the parade of customers and noncustomers and would-be customers, the stream of traffic. Turn around, and there's the store, with its new books and old favorites, the islands of display and canyons of shelves. For the browsing customer, the bookstore may be one errand in a hectic day, or a respite from that velocity, but for the bookseller, the store *is* the day, a stretch of time and space. Then the lull ends, and a customer approaches.

The deepest connections with customers usually come at the front counter, precisely because that island of counter between customer and bookseller creates an imaginative space for the two to occupy. There's the safety of the physical barrier, which allows both sides to be a little freer; you are close to each other, face to face, but a barrier remains. Both parties are free to leave at any moment, the clerk to her duties, the customer to the world.

But finally, it's the cash register that holds sway, for it implies the exchange of goods for money, and it's during these transactions that a bookseller learns the most about a customer. Out on the floor, it's all possibility, what a customer might choose to purchase, but at the counter, once the register starts ringing, that's where the revelations are. These are the books the customer will take home to read or stack up or offer as a gift, and each book, in some way, represents a part of that person's life. It's not a mere tally of reading tastes, who likes what authors, it's a gauge of what concerns people, what occupies them. There, face to face over the elbow-polished wood of the counter, bookseller and customer share a silent but telling moment. Travel guides, cookbooks, a book on divorce, one about ailing parents, a book of baby names, one about the horrifying spread of war in the new century, maybe the vampire novel that will take your mind off everything else, if only for twenty minutes at a time. It's a little like looking into another person's heart.

॥॥॥॥

Don't get me wrong, it's not always a warm, fuzzy adventure in retail, since the great American public can ask you for more than any store can hope to provide. Yes, in the back room of the bookstore, there's a lot of bitching about customers; sometimes, this is the only topic of conversation. Working with the public can be trying, anyone who's done it will certainly agree. But I do have a plan to change that, if I may digress.

In many countries military service is a mandatory obligation for citizens who've achieved their majority, and between the ages of eighteen and twenty, these young folk wear uniforms, march in battalion, study weaponry, and prepare to defend their country against invasion. In our country, to my eye, we've already got too much military (too many guns, at least, informally and otherwise).

I'd like to propose, modestly, a two-year mandatory retail service for all citizens and legal residents. No amount of family money or influence, or college dedication, would relieve you from this service. Mandatory; no exceptions. Only the luck of the draw would put you to work in a record store or a bookstore; the rest would have to work in the food industry or at the Gap, or heaven forbid, Wal-Mart. And for those lucky enough to pull book or record duty, the other advantage, aside from all the cool things you'd get exposed to and the free books and records (I show my age: CDs), would be the absence of a uniform.

This is the United States, after all, and as our national holidays make evident, the one thing we do best is shop. The benefits of mandatory retail service are, I think, many sided. The bank accounts of parents putting their children through college would be far less depleted by cell-phone charges, drinking games, and trips to Europe; these liberated funds could be invested to support our failed and failing corporations. Social Security coffers would grow. Because retail employees learn firsthand about the basic tools of business, colleges and universities would be able to restaff humanities departments with the money saved on accounting and marketing courses. Sales of sturdy shoes would skyrocket.

The greatest benefit to my little plan would be in the creation of a truly kinder and gentler nation. Imagine that every American citizen had at one time worked in retail, and you might glimpse the possibility of a future in which all of us, participating in our national pastime, shopping, would have more patience. We would understand that items are sometimes out of stock and life does continue, that service without a smile is still service, that getting rid of your small change is not one of life's more laudable goals, nor is cashing out a speed trial.

I'm going to let you in on a little secret about working retail. If you think we're grumpy, maybe even pissed off, and seem like we don't want to be there half the time—you're right.

Don't take this the wrong way. We may be curt with you, our valued clientele, but we're glad you've come to keep us busy, and we're still having a good time.

My proposal for mandatory retail service will never come to fruition, I'm certain, especially in a cultural climate where everyone yearns to be a rock star or a CEO, limousine riders all, but retail will survive, as it must, because there are enough of us out there who do—for one or two years, sometimes ten, twenty, or thirty—veer from the path of what we in the book trade call "real jobs." For the health of bookstores, there are enough of us who ignore the sign in the window: *Help wanted. Low pay, few or no benefits, questionable future, scant respect.* Those of us who sign up for the bookstore life seem to read between the lines: *Discounts on every book, flexible hours, inexplicably fun times, great camaraderie.*

It's a counter life we take on. Many booksellers, it turns out, aren't much suited for the more respectable callings.

IIIIII

On April 27, 1667, the poet and Puritan propagandist John Milton contracted with London bookseller and publisher Samuel Simmons for the rights to his new epic poem, *Paradise Lost.* Milton was to receive £5 in advance, and a further £5 when the first edition of 1,300 sold through. Although the book's cover price was only 3 shillings, *Paradise Lost* was a slow seller, and Milton didn't receive his second payment until 7 years later, just before he died. In 1680, Milton's widow sold all further rights to the poem to the same Samuel Simmons for a meager £8. *Paradise Lost* has remained in print for over 300 years, which is not a bad return on an investment of £18. This may be a typical publishing story—publisher takes on great book, author sells too short—but it marks the beginning of the age of the Author, and with that, the golden age of English bookselling.

In order for an author to become a public persona, a figure with authority, reach, and some small dram of integrity, there had to be booksellers to make him more than merely a writer. The difference between writers and authors, John Steinbeck once said, is that authors appear on the *Today Show*.

Until the late seventeenth century, most writers depended for their living on the luck of birth (independent wealth), or the financial kindness of superior strangers (patronage). During the Renaissance, some dramatists were able to eke out a living in the theatre, while still dependent on wealthy patrons for that extra cushion of comfort. Shakespeare's plays were published in his lifetime, but he didn't see one pence from them. Writers from antiquity on have chosen as their booksellers those who were most likely to spread their fame. In fact, many writers considered it *déclassé* to seek profits from their books. But the seventeenth century brought changes that would offer the writer a chance to make his living through his words, if perhaps a less than sumptuous living. There were more readers and writers, and avenues for publication increased accordingly. Late seventeenth-century Europe was awash in new journals, and there was a new place to find and read these journals, and to meet other readers. Coffeehouses became significant in spreading the advances of the Enlightenment.

Coffee came to Europe from the Middle East. Popular legend has it that an attacking Muslim army, rebuffed by Vienna's fortifications, fled quickly, leaving behind tons of beans, which the Viennese were able to turn into a thriving business. Historically, it's more likely that coffee simply arrived from the Arabic countries with imported goods at a time when Europe was once again trafficking with the world.

Although the plant originated in Ethiopia, the beverage coffee, or *qawha*, was not commonly used until the eighth or ninth century CE in Yemen, where Sufi worshippers drank it to help stay awake through the arduous hours of religious devotion. In the Middle East, coffee was also used as a medicine to cure any number of ills.

By the sixteenth century, the use of coffee had become commonplace in the Middle East, and the Arabic coffeehouse was a long-established cultural fixture. Patrons of early European coffeehouses would have recognized the style and intent of the Arabic coffeehouse. Customers were invited to stay for a long time and to engage in impassioned literary, political, and theological debates. One European observer of the Arabic coffeehouse called it a "theatre for the exercise of profane eloquence," and Ralph Hattox in his *Coffee and Coffeehouses* has

referred to it as "an excuse for sociable procrastination."
Same as it ever was.

The first English coffeehouse opened in Oxford in
1650 under the sign of the Angel in the parish of Saint
Peter of the East. This coffeehouse became a popular
meeting ground for students and professors loyal to the
then-deposed monarch, leading one Cambridge professor to posit that Oxford students might learn more in
the coffeehouse than by attending to their more formal
studies. Two years later in London, a public bill announced that coffee was now being "made and sold in
St. Michael's Alley in Cornhill, by Pasqua Rosée, at the
signe of his own Head." Rosée grew up drinking coffee
in his native Smyrna, and when he came to England to
join the service of a man named Edwards, Rosée introduced the drink to his English master and his London
friends, who were soon addicted to it and helped him
establish his business.

Within a few years, London was filled with coffeehouses, and the complaints came pouring in. An early
complaint, against James Farr at the Rainbowe by Inner
Temple Gate, was that he made a drink "of soote colour,
dryed in a Furnace, and that they drinke as hote as can
be endured." Neighbors called for the banishing of the
shop and its product because "he annoyeth his neighbrs.
by evil smells, and for keeping of ffier for the most part
night and day, whereby his chimney and chambr. hath
been sett on ffier, to the great danger and affrightment of
his neighbrs." Three of the petitioners were booksellers,

whose understandable fear of "ffire" kept them from spotting an early franchise opportunity. Keepers of ale-houses also complained, threatened by the sobering and less expensive coffee, but all complaints went unheeded. The coffeehouse conquered London, Paris, Vienna, Amsterdam, all the European capitals. Such was the popularity of this new institution that small change, farthings and pence, were suddenly unavailable in London, most of it sequestered in the tills of coffeehouse owners who were soon forced to mint their own tokens, which customers bought in bulk with larger bills, then doled out one at a time for single cups of coffee.

A timely addition to the evolution of the English coffeehouse was the introduction of tobacco from the Americas. The two new drugs formed a perfect recipe for the "sociable procrastination" of the coffeehouse, where one could now sit for hours, alternately buzzed up and mellowed out, talking with others under the same influences.

With the Puritan Revolution of the early part of the century and the continuing evolution of anti-Royalist sentiment throughout all of Europe, the coffeehouse appears at a time, on the eve of the Enlightenment, when commoner and landowner are beginning to mingle, where social barriers are being lowered. From its inception, the English coffeehouse is one of the most innovative and democratic forums in Europe; indeed, it is declared by law that anyone with the price of a cup of coffee may enter and strike up a conversation, no matter their social standing. Merchants, scientists, clergy, philosophers, dandies, all gathered here to engage in debates that would have been inconceivable fifty years earlier.

By fate, design, or accident, many of London's coffeehouses and booksellers found themselves in the same districts, often near Fleet Street and the Inner Temple Bar. Although there is no record of a combination bookstore/coffeehouse during this time, it's clear from the histories, both general and private, that the two have been allied, geographically and temperamentally, for a very long time.

|||||

A clothier may present the newest fashion trends, and by so doing, predict what people will wear, at least for the upcoming season. A bookseller, however, by virtue of what he sells, predicts how people will think, and changes in the way individuals think can bring about profound and long-lasting social effects. The booksellers of the Enlightenment did not only reflect their times, but helped to shape it. Without books to broadcast changes in thinking, history's ascent might have been a much ruder one. Because it changes what and how we think, the bookstore has always been a quietly powerful institution. But not always to the good of the bookseller.

What truly distinguished Printers Inc. from other great independent bookstores was our Computer section. Printers opened in the heart of the Silicon Valley in 1978, just prior to the first Silicon Valley Gold Rush. This was like opening a shovel shop in San Francisco in 1849, perfect timing. It seems hard to believe, but in 1978, less than thirty years ago, no one had a computer at home. At Printers, the computer books were technical and university publications so arcane in their information that only one of us on the staff, Rafael Diaz, even understood where they should be shelved within the Computer section. Although I had stolen the answers to my high school Algebra II final to pass the course, I knew math when I saw it, and that's what these books were—texts of endless equations with baffling alphanumeric titles. Rafael put little codes on each of the cards to help our decidedly literary staff. We placed the books on the shelves, and they flew off, at $65.00 a pop for some of the paperbacks. Word spread through the Silicon Valley, and our Computer section was soon as busy as the coffee bar.

Over the next twenty years, the customers of Printers' Computer section literally helped to create the demand for home computers, supercomputers required of government and academic research, computer and video games, virtual reality, the Internet, e-mail, and all the rest of the hard-wired software that both simplifies and confounds life today. The Computer section at Printers fueled the minds and imaginations of the architects of the second Silicon Valley Gold Rush, i.e., the dot-com bomb, and in so doing, also fueled, at least in part, the demise of Printers Inc. When the store closed in 2000, Printers had been steadily losing customers to the new electronic commerce, for here in the Silicon Valley, where the innovators of the computer industry had once come to Printers for the method and matter of their revolutions, the general trend, at the time, was away from the brick-and-mortar store, the physical space of the bookstore. You could shop on-line now; you didn't ever have to leave your house.

When Printers closed I drove to Palo Alto to bear witness. There was the big empty shoe box, white walls, and bad carpet. The only reminder of the former store was a red half-circle of linoleum where the coffee bar had once been. I peered into windows, wondering where all the noise had gone.

It's impossible to blame the closing of Printers on any one thing—certainly the fatigue of twenty years of small-business ownership took its toll on the owners—but it's undeniable that e-commerce was keeping people in front of their computers and out of the store. All of us book lusters who had worked at Printers had helped to build the future that was now leaving Printers behind. All we had left was empty space.

||||||

What's arresting about the English booksellers of the Enlightenment is that most of these merchants sprung from such low stations in life. On society's ladder, merchants were only slightly above pirates and other criminals. Here are some phrases used to describe London booksellers of the time: one is "the son of a drunken cobbler," another becomes a bookseller after "having narrowly escaped a university education," another comes to the profession after an apprenticeship in "several menial capacities," and one is "unpleasantly familiar with the prison-house." One bookseller came from so unpromising a background that he went into the profession in order to teach himself to read. We find one exception among these English booksellers: "He was different than other booksellers in that he was a rich man."

These booksellers were in many ways pirates, acting on the edge of a society still adjusting to new freedoms and ideas, yet looking to the bookstore as the source of these ideas. While laws were enacted to prevent the publication of seditious or obscene works, there was little policing, and public demand for new books continued to grow. The same was true with the copyright policies of the time; there were attempts at regulating the ownership of intellectual properties, but enforcement proved impossible. The bookseller as publisher produced a torrent of unofficial works, sometimes at risk to his bodily health.

Edwin Curll is the most notorious of these booksellers, a man who published the works of great poets and writers, though not always at their request. He also published popular and saucy titles, the ever-popular ribald romance—i.e., *Venus in the Cloister, The Nun in Her Smock, The Curious Wife*—as well as transcripts of government hearings, whose publication was explicitly forbidden. Such was his infamy that a new word arose— the sin of Curllicism. Curll also made a good living from publishing Bibles.

Curll was a tremendously successful bookseller, but he lived to pay for both his successes and his sins. For the publication of his obscene works, he was heavily and frequently fined, and while he managed to avoid prison, he was once subjected to an hour's humiliation in the public pillory in Charing Cross Road. Curll avoided the stoning and food pelting of the public during his hour in the stocks by printing and distributing a circular informing the public that he was in pillory for defending the memory of their beloved Queen Anne. Another time, after publishing a funeral oration by John Barber of King's College, without Mr. Barber's permission, Curll was seduced into the yard of the college by the promise of a more perfect copy of the oration; there, irate students tossed him roughly in a blanket for some long time (apparently a college tradition), then forced him to his knees to apologize to Mr. Barber.

The most notorious of Curll's punishments was concocted by the poet Alexander Pope, who showed a clever, if sickening, knack for revenge. Curll had published poems he falsely claimed were written by Pope. When Pope demanded a public correction and apology, he received only insolence from Curll. Pope then feigned to come to terms with Curll and invited him to the Swan Tavern in Fleet Street, where, along with Bernard Lintot, Pope's official publisher, the three men had drinks. Mr. Lintot, Curll records, had a half-pint of old hock, Mr. Pope a half-pint of sack, Mr. Curll the same. Pope secretly added a large quantity of emetic powder to Curll's drink, which soon caught up with him in the public street, a scene that Pope recorded for posterity in his mock epic *The Dunciad.*

Even the "prince of booksellers," Jacob Tonson, the son of a barber-surgeon from Holborn, was not above dubious practices. He once paid his best-selling poet and critic John Dryden in melons, and later complained that Dryden had given him more copy than Tonson had asked for and docked his advance accordingly. Still, Dryden was dependent on his bookseller, and not long after, he put aside his integrity to write and ask Tonson for more money, "I am much ashamed of myself that I am so much behindhand with you in kindness."

Despite his flaws, Tonson does represent the best of these booksellers and the contributions they made to the reading public. Tonson apprenticed himself, at fourteen, for seven years to Thomas Barnet, then opened his own shop in Chancery Lane under the sign of the Judge's head. At first, Tonson sold only secondhand books, but soon began publishing original dramatic works, quite unsuccessfully, until he became allied with Dryden, who was already known as the period's supreme man of letters. Together they published and promoted Dryden's work and helped to bring about—despite the melons—the age of the Author. Tonson had acquired, from Simmons, the rights to Milton's *Paradise Lost,* and it was his publication of the book that led to its popularity and acclaim. After moving out of the Chancery Lane shop, now operating under the sign of Shakespeare's head, Tonson was

also the first bookseller to make the Bard's plays and son-
nets widely available.

Tonson, Curll, and the other booksellers of the golden
age were opportunistic entrepreneurs, to be sure, but they
were key in shaping the literature of their time, a time of
profound societal changes.

|||||||

There is one other important physical development in
the seventeenth- and eighteenth-century bookstore, and
it's right in the front window.

When the bookstore was a stall, and later a three-
walled room, the shutters used to secure these shops at
night, were, when opened, used to display the shop's
wares. The books were placed face-out in the divisions of
the shutters. It was the same in Japan and China, except
that the shutters were taken off their hinges and laid on
the ground or a counter, and the books, arranged in neat
boxes on the inside of the shutter, were displayed face-
up. For centuries, the shutter was both wall and display.

As glass became more common and affordable, and
the bookstore more permanent, the shutters were replaced by glass windows that seduced customers with a
glimpse into the shop, offering close-up displays of new
books. Plate glass was a long way off, though, and many
booksellers found the smaller panes perfectly suited to
display. Tiny shelves were often built onto the backs of
the small windowpanes, so that the books would entice
curious passersby. Glass windows were used in other re-

tail shops, but there was such a natural correspondence between the size and shape of books and the small glass panes that such display innovations were far more common in bookstores.

However, booksellers soon discovered that such window displays faded the books, and so they deepened the bays behind the window, creating little stages in the store where the books could be shown to their advantage, and by so doing, offer an even larger view of the store from outside. Walking by most bookstores today, we find this arrangement, deep bays behind large windows, still in use after three hundred years, and the books still fading in the sun.

By the beginning of the nineteenth century, the book trade in England and Europe had become lucrative enough that most shops now sold the works of publishers other than themselves. The trade was even gaining respectability, alas, and drifting from its colorful roots. In 1794, James Lackington opened an enormous shop on the southwest corner of Finsbury Square in London called the Temple of the Muses. This was the first superstore, a two-story edifice with a glass cupola that lit the entire building. The store held over one million books: new and used, rare and antique, original manuscripts, and remaindered titles. The store also offered stationery supplies, bookbinding, and copy services. It was so large that at its grand opening a four-horse carriage paraded through the store. Bookselling had entered the realm of big business.

Big Business

The changes that shaped bookselling and publishing in the nineteenth century were, like those that shaped so much of that century, mechanical. In the first decade of the century, the Third Earl of Chesterfield, Charles Stanhope, introduced a printing press that looked much like Gutenberg's, but was made of iron instead of wood and was operated by levers rather than the traditional screw; these innovations added both speed and precision to the making of a page. In 1812, the Koenig printing press adapted steam power to a machine similar to Stanhope's, multiplying the number of pages printed per hour nearly fivefold. By 1890, two new methods of setting type—linotype, which forged an entire line of type at once, and monotype, which cast words one at a time—allowed composers to set five pages in an hour, as opposed to one and a half pages when set by hand, letter by letter. The pages of books were still sewn into signatures, which were then sewn together and laced into a cover, as they had been for centuries, but the binding process grew increasingly mechanized.

Which came first? Was the faster, steam-powered

printing press necessary because literacy rose so quickly during the Industrial Revolution, or did the literacy rate rise so fast because there was such a machine? They came into existence together, and the century overflowed with a variety and volume of newspapers, magazines, and novels impossible to conceive a hundred years earlier.

In the first decades of the century, in order to fill the demand of a growing urban populace, literate but without great means, the paperback came into being. These paperbacks, printed under the masthead of instant magazines or newspapers, were nothing more than popular novels that had been pirated by "unscrupulous" booksellers and publishers. In 1841, a German publisher introduced its Tauchnitz editions at one-third the price of leather-bound hardcovers. Railroads and steamships helped spread this bounty of literature, not only across a single country or language, but around the world.

One outcome of this machine speed, in the book trade and other industries, was a greater specialization of tasks, both for the individual worker and for entire organizations. For the bookstore, this increasing specialization meant that a bookseller was less likely to be a publisher, too. Faster, larger, and noisier machines were required to keep up with the explosion of printed matter, and it became less tenable for bookstores to keep printing presses in the back room. Frequently now the bookstore ordered from wholesalers and publishers, stocking a wider variety of the ever-growing catalogue of books.

For nearly two thousand years, the bookseller and

publisher had been one and the same, and for most of that time, a bookseller would carry only those works published on site. The change to a broader selection of books began in the American colonies, where printing presses were still few, as were booksellers, and there was a pressing demand for booksellers to import their stock from various English publishers. By the end of the nineteenth century, large American publishers still retained rather opulent flagship bookstores in their home cities, with their publishing offices often located above, but these shops now carried the works of many other publishers.

I was surprised to discover, during my first trip to Europe in 1986, that English and European bookstores were still arranged by publisher rather than by section; to find a book, you had to figure out the publisher first, then find that publisher's set of shelves. In the twenty years since then, however, most English and European bookstores have adopted the American system of shelving. Most of these stores now give out free bookmarks, another originally American device.

The twentieth century brought to bookselling the same advancements and pace-quickenings that urged along other industries. The rotary press, then later, electronic and computerized presses, along with more efficient distribution methods—interstate trucking and jet cargo— kept the business growing at a pace with the world's ever-growing literacy. Legal sanctions—improved copyright restrictions and fair trade practices—helped to stabilize and codify both publishing and bookselling.

The first profound revolution in twentieth-century bookselling was the introduction of the mass-market paperback just before World War II—Penguin Books in England and Pocket Books in the United States. The acceptance of the mass-market paperback was prompted by the war itself, when paper shortages made the purchase of these cheaper editions seem a patriotic act. The new paperback (the small pocket-size books one finds in airports and grocery stores as well as in bookstores) used less paper, and cheaper paper, and so saved more for the war effort. When a generation of soldiers returned from Europe and Asia, their G.I. Bills in hand, and flooded colleges and universities, they helped to sustain the demand for more affordable books.

The century's second revolution was the creation of the first national bookstore chains. In 1969, both B. Dalton and Waldenbooks opened their first stores, under parent companies of national department-store chains. Rather than maintain a presence in the carriage-trade shops of department stores, B. Dalton and Waldenbooks opened separate storefronts in the shopping malls that were then flooding the American landscape. In the same year, Little Professor opened its chain-franchise operation: individual owner-managers opened stores in towns and neighborhoods without bookstores.

There was a another paperback revolution in the 1980s, with the acceptance of the larger, trade-size paperback, and then further chainings in the 1980s and 1990s with Crown, Barnes and Noble, Borders, and others. During this time, publishing underwent, and continues to suffer under, a series of corporate conglomerations that have made many publishers only one segment of a global media empire. The story of bookselling in the twentieth century echoes the changing shape of capitalism.

Perhaps the biggest change in bookselling since the advent of big business is the loss of "characters." With increased speed and efficiency, the regulation of the industry, and most importantly, the separation of publishing from bookselling, the bookseller is no longer the rogue he once was and is rarely described as "unscrupulous." Those flamboyant personages of the golden age of English bookselling have all but disappeared from the more recent biographies and histories of the trade. Now we're talking business.

I'm saddened by this loss of color. Certainly there are "characters" in the trade still, but the same is true of any trade. Today's bookstores are mostly without notoriety, without edge. Today's bookstore is a quiet place, anonymous almost, homely, without glamour. At the same time I'm heartened to know that the bookstore can, and has, survived, and that it has changed only very slowly over three thousand years. This is part of the pleasure in visiting a bookstore, the knowledge that the simplest things do endure. The bookstore, the most common bookstore, unhyped and overlooked in our dazzling and dangerous world, remains essentially the same: the window of books that catches your eye, the front door like a novel's cover opened with great anticipation, the rows and shelves of waiting books, and the front counter, where a meager exchange of money for goods might do its magic once again. It's a business, but it's all about books.

|||||||

As the twentieth century has bent around into the twenty-first, many cultural coroners have announced the death of literacy. First, the novel "died" in the early 1960s, and then the bookstore itself "died" in the late 1980s. Now the very act of reading is dead, or at least in critical condition. Or so it's said. A 2004 study sponsored by the National Endowment for the Arts concluded that Americans were reading far less "literature," and far fewer "traditional" books than in previous decades. The Internet and electronic media, the study claimed, were taking Americans away from their books, in the same way radio and television provided distraction in years before. Woe be we.

But there are other figures that would argue against this claim, or at least offer some balance to it. In 2004, American publishers produced between 135,000 and 175,000 new titles, depending on the source. Let's settle in the middle, at 150,000 new titles every year, or around 411 new titles every single day. Each year American publishers produce 50,000 new titles more than what had been gathered in the entire nine-century history of the Great Library at Alexandria.

This figure also represents about 50,000 more titles than you'd find on the shelves of the largest bookstore. Most of a bookstore's space is devoted to backlist—i.e., titles previously published—so it's clear that bookstores of all stripes are needed to even begin to showcase every new book. What you see on the feature table of the most comprehensive bookstore represents the tiniest fraction of what's been recently published.

Some of these new titles are strictly professional and technical publications, still others are calendars, audio books, and books meant more as gifts than as objects to be read, but the majority are books in the traditional sense. Not every new book will have the lasting power of Aristotle's *Poetics,* but it's safe to say we won't be running out of things to read for a while.

There's a lot of catching up to do as well. *Books in Print* currently lists nearly 4 million active titles and 1.5 million out-of-print titles. Since 1980, over 2 million new books have been created, compared to the 1.3 million titles published in the preceding 100 years.

These are figures for American publishing alone. Americans do publish more books than any other country, but the per capita figure is surprisingly low. Of the English-speaking nations, the United States comes in fifth, behind the United Kingdom, Canada, New Zealand, and Australia. The United Kingdom publishes 2,336 books per person, the United States 545.

If you read one book a week, starting at the age of 5, and live to be 80, you will have read a grand total of 3,900 books, a little over one-tenth of 1 percent of the books currently in print. It may be premature for social critics to claim the death of the age of literacy; we're swimming in books.

‖‖‖‖

Out of this ocean of books, there is a small number that might be considered works of art. The fine-press tradition is a glorious one, but it's reserved for those with the passion and the money to sate that passion. I dare any lover of books to view the Arion Press edition of *Moby-Dick* without bursting into tears. The type is hand set, the paper handmade, the binding hand sewn. The leather of the book's slipcase and cover is as blue as the deepest ocean, and the Barry Moser boxwood engravings fairly leap off the page into the imagination, beginning with the first chapter's breaking wave and ending with the becalmed sea in which Ishmael floats, pondering infinity. A folio-sized book, its heft is powerful, in contrast to the soft, almost silky paper, in which, if you look carefully, you'll find the watermark of a whale. The book is a sensual overload even before the first sentence is read. Upon publication in 1979, it sold for $1,000, in an edition limited to 250 copies. Other fine-press books may be more or less expensive, and done in smaller or larger editions, but these books are intended for collectors.

Luckily for the rest of us, a trade edition of the Arion *Moby-Dick* was published in 1981, in a print run of thousands rather than hundreds, in both hardcover and paperback. The trade edition carries the same text and illustrations as the fine press, although it is smaller and machine produced. The trade *Moby-Dick* today costs a mere $29.95 in paper, $70.00 in cloth, and is a thing of beauty and a delight to read. But if $29.95 is still too dear, you can always buy a plain, mass-market paperback of *Moby-Dick* for $5.95, and find Melville's words and universal vision just as stunning. It is with the common book that most readers will spend their head-tilted hours.

|||||||

A bookseller frequently hears the same dismaying comment, "Well, I'd like to read it, but books are just too expensive." Considering that books might have cost 50 cents when you were a child, or that you might be able to find the same book for free in a library, then I suppose that a $25.00 hardcover novel does seem extravagant. But a little comparison shopping might help the recalcitrant customer rethink the book's long-term value.

Today a San Francisco movie ticket will set you back $10.00. Two hours later, give or take, and poof, that money is nothing but your memory, at least until you pony up another $20.00 for the DVD. A 400-page novel will probably take at least 8 hours to read. Once you buy a book, it's yours, and you can mark and look up at your leisure that one terrific paragraph that keeps floating through your head.

The technology of the book is much more flexible than film, more user friendly. The reader can dip into the book at will, without electricity, and is always aware of where she is in the book, halfway through, a third of the way, mere pages from the end, her fingers helping to measure the excitement of coming to the conclusion. Watching a scene from a film in slow motion is possible, but there's an unreal air to it; reading a passage from a book slowly does nothing to rob the words of their power. A film presents images; a book creates them inside the reader, with the reader's active participation. Books are good for your brain. Neurologists have found that, when watching television or film, the viewer's eyes remain idle, straight ahead, but when reading, the actual physical movement of scanning the page from left to right (or right to left, or up and down, depending) stimulates and conditions the brain, a Stairmaster of the mind.

The same $25.00 you'd spend on a hardcover novel could easily be spent for the entrée at a tony restaurant, salad, dessert, and wine not included. A terrific time is had by all, but the meal is quickly a memory. Chef Glenn Groening of Kezar Bar and Restaurant in San Francisco has created a duck breast over risotto—I claim it's one of the finests meals on the planet—and reasonably priced at $15.00, or roughly the price of a new trade paperback, but when I've finished the duck and want just a few more bites, as I always do, well, I'm out of luck unless I order another entire serving. Books are digested, Francis Bacon reminds us, but never consumed.

Even compared with a product as durable as shoes,

which may last a year of constant walking, the book triumphs again. In a given year, you probably won't read the same book as many times as you'd wear those shoes, but at the end of the year, the book will retain its freshness. A book does this even as the object itself begins to wear down. My *Collected Poems of Wallace Stevens* is twenty-five years old now, one of the most often read books in my library. The dust jacket is faded, torn at every corner, the binding loose, ink and pencil marks throughout, as well as coffee and food stains, but it still reads beautifully. Even a paperback printed on acidic paper, whose pages have yellowed ten years on, can still be read, no matter how badly the spine is cracked or how inflated it's become from being dropped in the bathtub. The pages might separate from the spine, but a rubber band can keep them together. You may loan a book to your circle of closest friends, but shoes are another matter. A great book will never go out of style—books go with every outfit.

The durability and flexibility of the book make it one of the most value-laden objects in the shopper's paradise we call America. This is surprising given that books are labor intensive to produce and expensive to ship and store. Your $25.00 price tag has to pay the writer, the bookseller, the publisher, and the printer, and the guy who drove the truck to deliver it. A publisher may be one person with cartons of books in his garage, or it may be an entire New York skyscraper filled with editors, marketeers, designers, production and sales staffs, and receptionists, not to mention a staffed warehouse, usually somewhere in New Jersey. The printer will support typesetters, machine operators of varying specialty, and shippers.

Let's look at your $25.00 hardcover and see where the money goes. We'll presume this is a non-best seller from a large New York imprint, a novel, say, so that, except for the dust jacket, no color or other special printing is involved. We'll give it a fairly average print run of 5,000 copies. Percentages will vary from book to book, from publisher to publisher, but the figures below are standard enough to paint the bigger picture.

Author	$ 1.88
Printer	$ 3.00
Publisher	$ 8.87
Bookseller	$11.25

The author's share of this pie seems, at first glance, ludicrously low, at least to authors. It is the smallest piece, but the one that's mostly likely to go to a single person. If the author has an agent, the agent receives between 10 and 15 percent of the author's royalties, but otherwise, the author gets to keep that buck-eighty-eight all to herself. Most writers will receive an advance against their royalties before the book is published, an advance based on the expected sales of that book. If you think writing will make you a millionaire, then you'd better write a book that the publisher hopes will sell over 500,000 copies. The royalty rate for a book that sells this much will be higher than that of a 5,000-copy hardcover, about $3.13 per book. In 2004, only 47 hardcover novels sold over 300,000 copies. A $16.00 trade paperback has an average royalty of $2.00 per book, and in 2004 only 27 trade paperbacks, fiction and nonfiction combined, sold over 500,000 copies. With mass-market paperbacks, the royalty is considerably lower, 42 cents on a $6.95 book, and you'd have to sell well over 2,000,000 copies to earn the fabled sum. In 2004, only 8 mass-market paperbacks sold this much or more. Your parents did not steer you wrong about the writing life: it's a hard way to make a living, almost impossible to get rich.

The largest slice of the $25.00 goes to the bookseller, but this figure is misleading if only the percentages are heeded. Out of the $11.25, the entire store's operation (payroll, rent, supplies) has to be supported, and there will be no film rights, serial rights, or other ancillary fees that conglomerate publishers depend on these days to balance their ledgers. In the end, a store can sell only so many volumes in a year, and sales totals will top out.

A large independent bookstore may have annual sales of $1,000,000 to $2,000,000, but the profit on these sales will be less than $100,000, leaning heavily to the zero end of the scale. A bookstore's annual profit can rest with the health of the Christmas season, and may come down to exactly how many calendars were sold, or how few days it rained or snowed during that time.

It's stunning to think that such a thing, a 400-page novel that you may pass on to your children, and they to theirs, can actually be yours for a scant $25.00. Books are not too expensive.

⠿

The German word for bookstore is *buchhandlung,* a place where books are handled. I vote we change the English world for bookstore to book-handlery because it's so fitting. The common book is made to be handled, as if the ultimate purpose for our opposable thumbs.

By the time a book reaches the bookstore, it's already been through many hands—writer to agent to publisher to editor to designer to printer to warehouse to sales rep to bookstore buyer. But when a book arrives in a store, its manhandled life truly begins.

First, the book is received. A medium-sized bookstore can receive 1,000 pounds of books each day, twice that during the Christmas warm-up, which starts in September. When a bookseller says, "We got a ton of books today," you can take his statement at face value. The receiving clerks in bookstores have the best jobs, I've always felt. There's relief from the daily barrage of customers and the always-exciting possibility of being the first one in the store to see the cool new books. The books are removed from their cartons, checked against the invoices, examined for damage, entered into the inventory, then readied to go out onto the floor.

The common book sports a good deal of information.

On the back of most books is a white rectangle with a series of numbers, a bar code, and other seemingly mysterious symbols. The bar code, a series of thin black stripes tattooed on nearly every retail item in the world, is capable of being read by a laser scanner for information: price, title, Universal Price Code (UPC), European Article Number (EAN), and more. I've always found it ridiculous that books have to be scarred by this glob of numbers and lines, given that so many are lovingly designed and produced. Other than the obvious advantage in monitoring the publisher's inventory, and sometimes the bookstore's, the hope of the bar code's presence, I assume, is that every book has the chance to become an international best seller and will soon be sold in Wal-Marts and price clubs along with that much needed six-pack of Tabasco sauce. I understand that it's a big corporate world out there, but I still hate that my new volume of Stephen Dobyns's poetry has the Big Brother stamp of approval. It's just not attractive. A simple ISBN number on the inside cover of each book would suffice for most inventory purposes.

Somewhere in this white rectangle is the ISBN, the International Standard Book Number, which identifies this edition of this specific title, and for most bookstores, this ten-digit number is enough information (although we're running out of ten-digit numbers, and ISBNs will get longer soon). The ISBN is grouped into four sections, each divided by a hyphen. The first section is always one number, and on American books that number is either 1 or 0. The numeral 0 used to indicate American books and 1 British books, but Americans made too many books, and so had to borrow from our Atlantic neighbors. The next set of numbers is the publisher's prefix, tying the book to its producer. You can tell how long a publisher's been around by the amount of numbers in a prefix; Harcourt's prefix, for instance, is only two digits, while a much newer publisher's prefix can be seven digits long. The third group of numbers indicates the specific title within a publisher's catalogue. The final digit in an ISBN is a check digit (sometimes the letter X rather than a numeral), which fulfills a mathematical formula verifying the number as a valid ISBN.

Many stores add information to a book by placing an adhesive tag on the back, one which holds inventory details specific to that store's computer inventory system, such as its proper section, thus allowing the store's computer to track sales patterns. The nice thing about these tags is that they can be peeled from the book without harming it. Mostly. Bookseller's tip: If you've peeled off an inventory sticker, or one of those annoying award stickers, and it's left a sticky spot on the book, put a dab of lighter fluid or window cleaner on a paper towel, rub delicately.

If the book is an expensive art book, the receiving clerk may seal it with a shrink-wrap machine, which encases the book in a thin plastic sheath that's blow-dried until it shrinks to a snug fit. Needless to say, the presence of a shrink-wrap machine in a bookstore's back room provides countless opportunities for goofing off, like shrink-wrapping someone's lunch or coffee cup. If the bookseller wants the dust jacket protected but the book still open, she might wrap the jacket in a paper-backed, clear plastic wrap called Brodart that's often found on library books. Can you Brodart that? is how it's verbed up.

The final step in receiving may be theft protection. A small strip of magnetized material is inserted into the book. With a hardcover, the strip, sticky on one side, is attached to a thin metal rod that's insinuated into the space between the book's spine and cloth cover. For paperbacks, a magnetic wire inside a thin strip of paper is stuck deep in the book's gutter, the narrow valley between pages. When this method was first introduced, manufacturers often printed the words "Complimentary Bookmark" in three languages on the paper strip, but that practice seems to have fallen off, probably because no one believes a piece of paper 1/8" wide makes a proper bookmark. If a customer tries to leave the store without paying for the book, or if the clerk forgets to swipe the book's spine over the de-magnetizing device, the alarm gates at the front door will sound.

Once all this is accomplished, the books are put on a cart or table, ready to begin their shelf lives.

Depending on the size of the store, a book may first arrive in a stack of 5, 10, 25, 100, or more. Perhaps this book has promise and will immediately go to a feature table or shelf to be displayed with other new arrivals. The feature table or shelf may include new books from all sections, only hardcovers, trade paperbacks, mass-markets, fiction, nonfiction, or all the new cookbooks.

If there are 25 books, 5 or 10 will go on this table,

where another title has sold out and left a gap. Or room will have to be made, and the stack of last week's promise that didn't pan out will be removed to make way. Several other copies will be put on the shelf in that book's section, most likely with the book face-out, and the rest will be put in backstock. Booksellers don't so much count the books on feature tables, as measure them—hey, that stack was a hand's span higher yesterday. A book has about a week to start selling before it gets consigned to the cramped shelves of its subject section because, after all, we did just receive a ton of new books and they look pretty good. If a book sells immediately, thanks to reviews, word of mouth, expectation, cover beauty, enticing title, author's name, or sheer luck, it can stay featured as long as it sells.

Once the feature life of a book is over, it may still have legs when moved to its section, where the book waits to be looked for or stumbled upon. Putting a book onto a shelf can require some work. There are just too many books here, and if the shelf is stuffed, both brute force and logic may be called upon. First and easiest question, are there any face-outs that can be turned spine-out to provide more space? If the shelf is tight but has some give between Bulgakov and Buzzati, the bookseller can make it work. The best method is to pull the last Bulgakov and the first Buzzati halfway out, then slide the new book between them, and gently nudge. Sometimes there's no give, and to make space, the bookseller may have to spine out a title three shelves below, move two books from the second to the third shelf, move five really skinny books from the first to the second shelf, and find the space for the new book there. And on and on. As solid and heavy as the bookstore seems, it's fluid, too, always in motion.

Anytime after its first three months in the store, a book can be returned to the publisher for credit. Returns are an important aspect of the book trade, for they do allow the bookseller to take a chance without too much risk. But the cost of postage to return books to the publisher, which the bookseller pays, eats into a bookstore's cash. Returns place a burden on the publisher as well, a constant problem in the business that no one has yet overcome. If our stack of twenty-five books hasn't sold after three months, the bookseller may return all copies, or keep a few. Books returned to a publisher may be sold to another bookstore as new books. Anytime a book is shipped, shelved, and packed for return, it's going to show wear. If you've ever bought a new book that looks as if it's been halfway around the world, you might be right.

Let's imagine, sadly, that most copies of a book were returned to the publisher, and the publisher still has 3,000 of the 5,000-copy first printing. These days, if a book doesn't sell quickly enough, it's often declared out of print by the end of its first year, lightning fast for such a slow business. But this does not mean that the book's life in the bookstore is over. Publishers sell the remaining stock of an out-of-print book, for pennies on the dollar, to companies that specialize in remainders. The remaindered book reappears in the bookstore with a sticker that says "Was $25.00 Now $6.98." Remainders are a boon for the bookstore because they're discounted deeply, 50 percent and above, and don't require tight inventory control. The publishers can recoup something of their loss. The poor author, though, is out of the loop, for no royalties are paid on remainders; however, remainders can act as an advertisement for the author's next book. For the customer, it's gold. That book you saw last year and really wanted but couldn't afford— here it is, and less than half the original price. Yowza! Now you can buy more books.

‖‖‖‖

On the feature table or hidden in its section, the book, though much handled already, is just beginning its life. The customer spots it, something clicks, and she picks it up. Maybe she carries it around the store, picks up three or four other books, sits down in the ragged velour easy chair, and looks through them while sipping a latté. Yes, she'll take the first one. If she's a well behaved customer, she'll put the unchosen ones back in their proper places. Then to the register.

From here the book has many possible futures. It can be devoured immediately on getting home, even taken straight to a café for more immediate gratification. Maybe the reader will take a few peeks at the first couple of pages while waiting at the stoplight. Once home, the book may go on top of the pile of those still waiting to be read, or to the bottom, where it can stay for years. In my stack of unread books right now, I've got a history of the Danube River by Claudio Magris and a scientific study on the patterns of global migration, DNA, and languages. I would like to read these books, but they've become part of the furniture. Maybe next year, after I finally get to *The Aeneid*, a twenty-years-ago purchase that has been moved to my permanent shelves.

Or the book might be a gift. Books do make perfect gifts, but by their very nature, books can also be a problem as tokens of affection. The delay factor is huge. Ask any of my godkids or nieces and nephews. Oh, look, they've been heard to say, another book from Uncle Lew, gee, what a surprise, thank you. I can't help myself, I have to give them books. You can thank the gift giver for the gesture, but true thanks for the book have to wait until it's been read.

It's always dicey choosing that gift book, too. You may have loved it, but your close friend, unbeknownst to you, doesn't find books about talking Minotaurs that exciting. This is something akin to giving a sweater that's the wrong size, except that there are 3.7 million sizes to choose from. A book gift can be a difficult transaction for both parties; the recipient doesn't immediately know what to say, the giver may have to wait months or years for the final thank you. Awkward silences ensue.

Don't let any of this stop you, though. Pick books with beautiful covers, so you'll get that first ooh and ahh, and understand that a new book, precisely because of its durability and ubiquity, can always be exchanged for the one they truly desired.

|||||||

The book's been made, bought, and read happily, but its shelf life isn't necessarily finished yet. As a bookseller and a rep, I've had many more thousands of books in my possession than my shelves at home would indicate. At one time, I tried to keep them all, but that quest soon became impossible; I now only keep the ones I'm sure I'm going to reread, the ones I'm definitely going to read before I die, and the ones I can't bear to part with because of an aesthetic or emotional attachment. If my wife and I hadn't gone short-shelf, keeping only those books we're certain we will reread, there'd be no room for my daughter, to say nothing of her books. And so we have visited the used bookstore frequently in the last eight years.

What a wonder is the used bookstore. You take in books you've loved, books that have bored you, books that are ratty looking, and you get cash or credit with which to buy more books. If it's a combined new and used store, like the vaunted crazy castle of San Francisco's Green Apple, then the lugging of those boxes across town makes the trip worth the back strain. I can convince myself I've actually saved money, pick up the new Philip Roth, and buy a sweet leather-bound edition of Marcus Aurelius's *Meditations,* and still save the last of the credit for my next trip. Okay, fine, I'll use the whole credit today.

For me, one of the great things about selling my books

is that I know the ones I've sold can now begin an entire new existence. No longer relegated to my shelf or worse, a box in the garage, these books can go to a new home, possibly staying forever, possibly being traded in once again. How curious to come upon a previous owner's name on the inside cover of used book, even more so if that reader has added marginalia—"too depressing!" "love this," "what?" Who was this other person who inadvertently shared with me the pleasures of this imagined world? Or the story that's found in the romantic dedication on the flyleaf—"Dear Bobolink, may you always cherish this book and have me next to you when you open it, love, Cliff." Whatever happened to Bobolink and Cliff anyway, what went wrong?

The first time I found one of my own books in a used bookstore, only a month or so after it was published, I was momentarily dismayed (devastated, actually). Was it such an uninspired novel that someone had traded it in after the first few pages? A closer look told me that it had been read, the spine was cracked, the pages curled. This fact didn't immediately assuage my shame; even though read, it might have been read with a sneer and a yawn. But slowly I began to appreciate, as I suppose I had to, the great continuity of the used bookstore, how it keeps alive and in motion those books that otherwise might have to be burned for an Egyptian's bathhouse fuel. Used bookstores represent recycling at its best, a powerful and useful endeavor that's important to both our cultural and material lives.

Even the used bookstore has its limits, though, and

must clear out the poor orphans. First, there's the dollar bin, usually a table or cart outside the front door, where certain books are priced to move at fifty cents or one or two dollars. Don't overlook the dollar bin because it's not always about lack of quality. I recently found a nice hard-cover of Doctorow's *Ragtime* for $1.00 at Green Apple. I'd always meant to read it, and I did. For a lousy buck.

After the dollar bin comes the free box, usually on the ground and often filled with out-of-date textbooks. I like to keep an eye on the local free box, noting what's in it, and checking again a few days later, only to find that the 1963 manual on arc welding has disappeared, along with every other pamphlet and old magazine.

Last week, I found a copy of the essayist Loren Eisley's *The Immense Journey* on top of a garbage can at the busiest intersection in my neighborhood. It's a first edition, with a jacket, and in fine shape. Published in 1957, it appears never to have been read. The book was on top of a stack of other books, and in good urban fashion, was obviously meant to be taken, but I looked around with a strange sense of guilt, as if I were about to steal something. My wife and I both love Eisley and had been talking about him just the week before, but we don't have a copy of this one. The book was inches away from an ignominious end, so I snatched it up and brought it home.

Not *My* Doolittle You Don't

Why do people go into bookselling? It's not for the money, or the glamour, or a secure future. The answer is simple: love. You love books so much that you believe a book, any book, is an important object, nearly sacred. You also believe that the free trade of those books is key to a society's democratic nature. On a day-to-day basis, this lofty emotion can get lost in the paperwork barrage and unending carts of books to be shelved. There are times, however, when a bookseller's beliefs are truly put to the test, times when individuals or institutions attempt to eradicate certain books or control the public's ability to obtain them.

For most of its history, the bookstore has remained free of the constraints of government regulation. Writers and publishers have often suffered under explicit censorship, but the bookstore itself, in part because it appears to be a mere store rather than a powerful force in society, has been ignored. Anonymity has its rewards. The biggest exceptions to this benign neglect were those bookstores in the Soviet Union, and today the bookstores of the People's Republic of China. Communism, derived from and fed by books perhaps more than any other type of government, seems to have understood from the beginning that it would have to control the distribution of books, as well as their writing and publication, if it were to control the hearts and minds of its citizens. Both Soviet and Chinese bookstores were established and controlled by the government; the downside to this is, of course, a severe limitation on what books were actually made available to the public, but the upside was that those books that were available, subsidized by the governments, were cheaper than those books in the West. Still, how many novels about heroic tractor drivers can one read? Only in recent years has U.S. intrusion into bookstores become policy rather than aberration.

And because the bookstore has also remained—again, for the most part—a mom-and-pop, little- or no-profit institution, it's also remained free of the pressures of corporate graphs and margins. Until the 1990s, with the advent of the superstore chains and Amazon.com, there simply wasn't been enough money in bookselling to make it worth Wall Street's attention.

These freedoms, from governments and corporations, have created a unique position for the bookstore, from the time a bookseller first put down a carpet and displayed his wares through to the present day. Able to sell anything, booksellers have sold everything, including those works that threaten and offend others. Over the centuries, the bookstore has continually found itself a stronghold of the rights of free expression.

||||||

In March 1989, I spent a weekend at Gallery Bookshop in the small town of Mendocino on California's north coast. I was a sales rep at the time and had become friends with shop's owner, Tony Miksak. Tony had invited a few sales reps, some friends of the store, and the interested public to spend the weekend in the store's rather cramped space. Throughout that rainy weekend, we gathered around the wood-burning stove, huddled on the floor and in the few chairs, and read aloud to one another. In bookstores around the country, the same scene was repeated. In Mendocino and elsewhere, we all wore big white buttons with black lettering: "I am Salman Rushdie."

Only a few weeks earlier, on Valentine's Day, Iran's Ayatollah Khomeini had declared a *fatwa* on Salman Rushdie, a death sentence that offered a reward of £1,000,000 for Rushdie's assassin. The Ayatollah and the senior clerics of Iran were offended by passages from Rushdie's new novel, *The Satanic Verses,* and claimed the book to be an act of heresy against their god. The book had ignited an international furor since its publication; even before the *fatwa,* members of the Muslim community in one Indian city burned copies of the novel, rioted, and called for the author's death. After the *fatwa* was declared, Rushdie went into hiding, under the cloak of the British Secret Service. All because of a novel, a story, a fable, a fiction, an admitted lie.

The *fatwa* was unique. Books have always been bowdlerized, banned, and burned, for every conceivable reason.

Writers and their publishers have been prone, under a variety of circumstances, to being exiled or imprisoned for their writings. But the public call for Rushdie's death, with the offer of a substantial reward, raised the stakes. Rushdie was a cosmopolite, a citizen of the world, but after the *fatwa* he was not safe in any country. The *fatwa* also called for the deaths of those who published and distributed the book.

Around the world, individuals, organizations, and governments protested the *fatwa* and called for it to be rescinded, but press conferences rarely change anything. The international book community, publishers and booksellers alike, immediately rushed to the book's defense, determined to make the book prosper by putting it into the hands of as many readers as possible. Security was tightened at the offices and warehouses of the book's publisher, and new print runs were ordered.

But the climate was dangerous in ways no one could predict. On February 26, a crowd of 10,000 pro-Ayatollah demonstrators gathered in front of the United Nations in New York City and demanded Rushdie's death and the eradication of his novel. On February 28, firebombs were thrown through the windows of Cody's Books and a Waldenbooks, both in Berkeley. Similar incidents occurred around the world in the following months, and bookstores, book wholesalers, and publishers received thousands of anonymous threats. Interestingly, most of the threats in the United States came from the State of Oklahoma, from white non-Muslims.

The book trade's reaction was not entirely unanimous. Several large chains either withdrew the book from their stores, or withdrew it from the shelves, forcing customers to ask for it. The corporate managers of the chains cited employee safety, a gesture that seems reasonable today, but within a month or so, these chains reinstated the book. Writers, independent booksellers, and concerned citizens had protested at several chain-store locations, which may have had an effect on the policy, but what eventually changed the policy was flagrant noncompliance by employees at individual stores, and repeated requests by these employees to put the book where it belonged, on the shelf.

Independent booksellers were not unanimous in their response either, but within a week of the *fatwa,* the vast majority were prominently displaying and promoting the book, wearing "I am Salman Rushdie" buttons, and holding in-store marathon readings. The book began to sell, in larger quantities than anyone expected, and several stores posted huge signs in their front windows, "*Satanic Verses* Sold Out, Order Yours Today." The book became an international best seller.

The wearing of a button or the hanging of a sign are at best symbolic acts, but such gestures do call attention to an issue and help spread the news, and can create a sense of unity among the believers. What's most important about the book trade's response to the Rushdie *fatwa* is that, even in the earliest weeks of the *fatwa* when no one knew what to expect, the bookselling community took a stand. We held the dangerous book in our hands, we brought it into our stores, we made sure the forces of silence would not prevail.

||||||

Since the nineteenth century, when the divide between publisher and bookseller widened, there have been many occasions when a bookseller has had to supplant the role of the publisher and become, as in earlier times, the source of important literary works that others would not take on. On most of these occasions, the bookseller has had to publish the work because publishers were afraid to do so.

On November 17, 1919, a thirty-two-year-old American named Sylvia Beach opened the doors of her new bookshop at No. 8 rue Dupuytren in Paris's Left Bank. Despite the grandeur of its name, Shakespeare & Co. was a modest affair. Borrowing $3,000 from an aunt in New Jersey, Beach converted a former laundry into a one-room English-language bookshop and lending library, whose centerpiece was the laundry's old fireplace. Most of the store's stock, and all of its furniture, were scavenged from the flea-market stalls of Paris's St.-Ouen. Just as the store was set to open, Beach and her bookselling mentor Adrienne Monnier noticed that the sign painter had made a mistake. "Book Hop" was clearly painted next to the front door, but there was neither time nor money to change the sign, and the typo, which Beach found appropriate to her new venture, remained.

If the accommodations were modest, Beach still had grand designs for her shop. She had no experience in bookselling, nor in any previous business. The daughter of a well-to-do Presbyterian minister, she had lived with her family in Paris as a teenager, where she developed a passion for the city; she returned in 1916, along with the first wave of American expatriates who would come to be known as the Lost Generation. Her childhood in a family of devoted readers had given her a ferocious passion for books, and somewhere in adolescence, she developed a vague notion that she might one day open a bookshop. Beach's particular literary interests were the English and American Modernists then transforming the notion of what literature could be—among them Gertrude Stein, Ezra Pound, William Carlos Williams, and her literary idol, James Joyce.

Setting out, with no experience, to open a specialty foreign-language bookstore, whose patrons were to be starving artists and writers, Sylvia Beach could not have guessed that, not only would she succeed in her venture, but that she would come to the rescue of one of the twentieth century's great novels.

‖‖‖‖

Shakespeare & Co. immediately became a gathering place for the artists of the Left Bank: English, American, French, and otherwise; writers, painters, and musicians. Beach designed the shop as a comfortable place, encouraging her customers to stay awhile. Shelves lined the walls, but the main area of the shop was more like a living room, filled with overstuffed couches. Images of and by writers filled every inch of wall space—photos of Walt Whitman and Edgar Allan Poe, and Beach's favorite contemporaries and customers, along with two original line drawings by William Blake. When new writers visited Shakespeare & Co., they were invited to hang their photos on the walls, a clever bit of marketing on Beach's part, insuring, through vanity, return customers.

Beach stocked the most progressive of the day's literary journals—the *Little Review, Broom,* the *Dial, This Quarter, Poetry,* the *Egoist,* the *New English Review*—as well as the current poetry and fiction that she gathered on buying trips to London. Like many bookshops before the middle of the twentieth century, Shakespeare & Co. was also a lending library, where customers could subscribe for three, six, or twelve months for the privilege of borrowing three books at a time for up to three weeks. Gertrude Stein was one of Beach's original subscribers, but threatened to withdraw her subscription when she discovered the shop did not carry the classic children's novels *The Trail of the Lonesome Pine* and *The Girl of the Limberlost;* Stein only changed her mind when Beach reminded her that the store *did* carry books by Gertrude Stein.

Shakespeare & Co. became that home-away-from-home the Lost Generation required, and for many, Beach's bookstore was the only mailing address they would have in Paris, and the one place they could be certain of running into friends. The mail was kept in a heap on the fireplace mantel, next to the framed mirror that displayed photos of the store's favorite children and pets, until one day it all became too much. A friend of the store donated a set of pigeonholes salvaged from a bank, and thereafter, the mail was sorted alphabetically. It had become official, Shakespeare & Co. was the heart of the Paris literary scene, which meant, during these years, the heart of the world's.

The list of writers who were regulars at Shakespeare & Co. during its twenty years is formidable: André Gide, Paul Valéry, Sherwood Anderson, F. Scott Fitzgerald, Ernest Hemingway, D.H. Lawrence, Gertrude Stein and Alice B. Toklas, Ezra Pound, Samuel Beckett, and James Joyce.

||||||

Sylvia Beach had read Joyce's *Portrait of the Artist as a Young Man* in 1914, when she was still in Princeton with her family. Convinced of Joyce's genius, she began to follow his work, including those portions of his new novel, *Ulysses,* that appeared in the *Little Review* between 1918 and 1920. It was through serendipity, however, that she came to meet her literary hero.

Adrienne Monnier, who owned a French bookshop around the corner from Shakespeare & Co., had been invited, via Mr. and Mrs. Ezra Pound, to a supper party given by one of Pound's protégés, André Spire. Monnier, no fan of Spire's poetry, begged Beach to come along.

The host whispered to Beach that the Irish writer James Joyce was at the party, and for the briefest of moments, Beach was so anxious at the prospect of meeting him, she nearly ran off. After a dinner during which Joyce did nothing but keep his wineglass from being refilled, to the amusement of the French hosts, Beach found the great writer hiding in the library, slouched between two bookcases, reading. They spoke of Joyce's recent move from Trieste, his work on *Ulysses,* and his fear of stray dogs.

Joyce stopped by the next day, July 12, 1920, and would spend much of the next ten years in the shop. Sylvia Beach was by all accounts a comforting and disarming presence—minutes after meeting Hemingway, he was showing her his battle scars—and on that first day at Shakespeare and Co., Joyce told her all about his financial troubles, his worsening glaucoma, and the design of his new novel. Before he left that day, he became a subscriber to Shakespeare & Co.'s lending library—for one month. A longer subscription was beyond his budget. Joyce was often in the bookshop after this, cashing checks, doing research, and complaining about his attempts to get *Ulysses* published.

After the critical success of *A Portrait of the Artist as a Young Man,* the literary world waited anxiously for Joyce's next work, a work he himself professed would be one of genius, a genius beyond even that of his last. When portions of *Ulysses* first appeared in the *Little Review,* the magazine's subscribers and critics, and its printers, too, began to object. It was obscene, many said, and no

British publisher had the courage to acquire the novel. In America and in Britain, copies of the *Little Review* were confiscated and burned by postal and customs authorities. The journal's editors, Margaret Anderson and Jane Heap, vowed to publish the entire book under their own imprint, but could find no American or English printers willing to take on the job. At the time, if a book were found illegal on grounds of obscenity, both the publisher and the printer could be held liable; *Ulysses* had already created too much of a stir to avoid notice.

In 1920, the New York Society for the Suppression of Vice, led by John S. Sumner, filed a complaint in a New York courtroom, and the *Little Review*'s Anderson and Heap were brought to trial on obscenity charges for publishing the Nausicaa section of *Ulysses.* During the portion of the trial when sections of the novel were read aloud, one of the three white-haired judges asked that the courtroom be cleared of all ladies, at which point the defense attorney, John Quinn, had to remind the judge that the ladies present in the courtroom were the defendants, the publishers of the obscene material. Surely, the judge argued, the "young ladies" could not have known what they were doing.

The outcome of the trial was never much in doubt. Even John Quinn admitted he was no fan of Joyce's and bluntly told his clients they were sure to lose. The best courtroom defense he could muster was that *Ulysses* was not literature at all, that it was "gobbledy-gook," unintelligible to the average adult, and therefore could not be obscene. He may have been uninspired as an attorney, but Quinn was a savvy investor. During the trial he arranged, through Sylvia Beach, to purchase the manuscript of *Ulysses* as it was written, paying Joyce a fair price for the pages, which he was certain, and rightly so, would become much more valuable in the future.

On February 21, 1921, Anderson and Heap were each fined $50.00 and instructed to refrain from publishing further excerpts from *Ulysses*. It took until the end of March for Joyce to learn the outcome of the trial, and he immediately went to Shakespeare & Co. to talk the matter over with Beach. In the year they'd known each other, Beach had become one of Joyce's most trusted confidants; Joyce, a shy and greatly formal man, was taken by Beach's intelligence and honesty, and also by her decorum. Knowing that all English publishers were closed to Joyce, Beach rashly proposed that Shakespeare & Co. take on the novel.

‖‖‖

Shakespeare & Co.'s original prospectus for *Ulysses* claimed the novel would be available in the fall of 1921, but this proved an optimistic deadline for such a difficult book.

First, there were customers to be found. The book was to be a limited edition of 1,000 copies, 100 on Dutch handmade paper, 150 on Verger d'Arches paper, 750 on a standard handmade paper, all editions bound by delicate paper wrappers in the French tradition. But at 350, 250, and 150 francs respectively, *Ulysses* would surely be the most expensive paperback ever. Friends of the bookshop signed up, and subscriptions were sold throughout Paris by writers and artists who took blank order forms with them to atelier parties.

The printing and typesetting of the book was a task as monumental as the novel itself. Beach, through her friend Monnier, contacted a Dijon printer, Maurice Darantière, if only out of anti-English snobbery. One of the biggest problems with the book's production was that French typesetters had to set, and by hand, one of the most challenging novels ever written in English, a language in which they were not competent. Darantière, a Master Printer of several generations, persevered with the job, even though he had taken it on speculation. He knew he would not be paid, if ever, until the subscription money leaked in.

The primary difficulty with the printing of the novel would prove to be Joyce himself. Joyce's manuscripts of the novel are nearly impenetrable, and he continued to make changes, vast changes, as the novel was being typed by English secretaries in Paris. The novel, over seven hundred pages typeset, went through nine different typists during the eleven months of preparing the manuscript. One of the typists, after only a few days, knocked on Joyce's door, and in tears, threw a batch of manuscript pages at him and stormed off before she could be paid. After the pages were typed and sent to Darantière for setting, Joyce continued to make changes on the proofs of the novel, in a handwriting that was deteriorating along with his eyesight. Joyce later estimated that fully one-third of *Ulysses* was written on the typeset proofs, proofs only Sylvia Beach was allowed to translate for Darantière.

Joyce became convinced, and Beach agreed, that the novel's paper wraps should be the exact colors of the Greek flag, white type on blue paper. The blue had to be an exact match, representative as it was for Joyce of the Homeric nature of the novel, and the tradition of free speech in Attic Greece. Joyce and Beach traveled throughout France in search of the proper color, only to discover that a costly lithography process was needed to ensure an exact match.

In the middle of all this, Beach moved her bookshop, always a difficult and dusty task, but in this case also a great boon to Beach. The new store, at No. 12 rue de l'Odéon, was just around the corner from the old shop, but considerably larger—two rooms—and directly across from Adrienne Monnier's French bookshop. Beach and Monnier had become increasingly close. Monnier had publishing experience, and in this and all other aspects of the book business, she was a devoted mentor and friend to Beach.

Finally, though many months late, the final proofs were ready. Joyce's fortieth birthday, 2.2.22, a date deemed propitious by both Joyce and Beach for its numerological symmetry, was approaching quickly, and Beach hoped to present a finished copy of the book to its author on this day. A week before, Darantière had told Beach this would be impossible, he would need several more weeks to produce a finished copy, but Beach pressed Darantière, and on the evening of February 1, she received a telegram instructing her to meet the 7 a.m. express train from Dijon. That morning at Gare du Nord, Sylvia Beach was handed a small package containing two finished copies of *Ulysses.*

Beach took the first copy to Joyce, the second she put in the window of Shakespeare & Co. By the time the shop opened the next morning, a crowd of the book's subscribers had gathered, clamoring for their copies. They had to wait another six weeks.

⦙⦙⦙⦙⦙⦙

The distribution of *Ulysses* to overseas subscribers was going to be difficult, Beach knew. Postal and customs authorities in both the United States and England would certainly hear of the publication and be on the lookout for the infamous novel. Joyce wisely suggested to Beach, on the day the first large shipment of books arrived from Darantière, that they immediately ship out all copies bound for England and Ireland before word could spread, and so the two sat down in Shakespeare & Co. that day and wrapped and addressed several hundred individual copies. James Joyce was a genius, but he was no bookseller. In attempting to glue labels to packages, Joyce got so much of the glue and bits of label stuck to him that Beach had to cut pieces from his jacket and his hair. Both Joyce and Beach were delighted to learn that the book weighed one kilo five hundred and fifty-five grams, another propitious number. And they were both thrilled with the heft and look of it, a simple but elegant book: the title in white type near the top, the author's name at the bottom, and the cover the perfect shade of Greek-flag blue.

Getting the book to American subscribers would be another matter, as news of the publication would certainly arrive before the first ship. Another Shakespeare & Co. regular, Ernest Hemingway, devised a plan. Hemingway's Chicago friend Bernard B. (whose real name is still a secret) would rent a studio apartment in Toronto. Canadian officials wouldn't be expecting the book, it had yet to become an issue there. Once copies of the book arrived in Toronto, Bernard B. began to take the ferry to the United States with one copy of *Ulysses* tucked safely in his pants. This took several months, and near the end, as Bernard B. became uneasy, he enlisted a friend to help, and each day the two of them, with two copies each tucked in their trousers, crossed over from Toronto.

Other shipments of the novel in the first and subsequent editions were discovered at various borders, where they were confiscated and burned. For twelve years, Shakespeare & Co.'s was the only legitimate edition, and even the several pirated editions that floated around Europe were based on Beach's original. Sylvia Beach eventually printed over 10,000 copies, and during all those years, she faced a constant struggle to get the book safely to its readers.

The second week of December 1933 was a big one for repeals in the United States. Prohibition was officially concluded, and on December 6, Judge John M. Woolsey of the United States District Court, New York, lifted the ban against Joyce's novel. Two months later, Random House, who had instigated and paid for the appeal, published the first general trade edition of *Ulysses*. Beach was relieved to have the burden of the novel off her shoulders and delighted to know that the book was free to travel the world. While Joyce had been paid all along for the book, and more in the way of small loans and advances, Beach finally made some real money off the book, too.

‖‖‖‖

Shakespeare & Co. stayed open for a little over twenty-two years, closing in December 1941. The Germans had occupied Paris in June 1940, but Beach, like many Parisians, had decided to stay, to remain as one of the caretakers of the city and its way of life.

One day that December a high-ranking German officer pulled up in front of the little shop at No. 12 rue de l'Odéon and told Beach he would like to purchase Joyce's newest novel, *Finnegans Wake,* a copy of which was displayed in the store's front window (*Finnegans Wake* was published in 1939, in the United Kingdom by Faber and Faber and in the United States by the Viking Press). The officer was a great fan of English literature, he said, and of Joyce in particular. He believed the book would help him with his command of English idioms.

Beach told the officer that she could not sell it, it was her last copy, her personal copy, and when the officer left, she hid the remaining copies of the book.

A week later the same officer returned, again demanding to purchase *Finnegans Wake*. No, Beach told him, they had run out, she was so sorry. The officer threatened to return later that day and confiscate everything in the shop if she did not comply, but Beach held her ground, and the officer left.

Beach immediately went to her landlord and arranged to take possession of an unoccupied flat on the building's fourth floor, and for the next several hours, Sylvia Beach and Adrienne Monnier, aided by friends, moved every book, five thousand in all, along with the magazines, photographs, and furniture, up four flights of stairs. They disguised the entrance to the hidden apartment, then painted over Shakespeare & Co.'s name and address, and watched from Monnier's shop when a confused German patrol showed up to loot the then-vacant store. The contents of Shakespeare & Co. remained hidden until after the liberation of Paris, but the store never reopened.

|||||

Each year during the last week of September, the book trade celebrates its struggle against censorship with Banned Books Week. Since 1982, bookstores and libraries around the country have displayed banned books and held events to inform the public about books, mostly fiction titles, that have been the target of censorship, and how such attacks on free expression might be curtailed or stopped. Banned Books Week is sponsored by the American Booksellers Association, American Booksellers Foundation for Free Expression, American Library Association, American Society of Journalists and Authors, Association of American Publishers, National Association of College Stores, and is endorsed by the Center for the Book at the Library of Congress. Amnesty International has joined the fray with a concurrent Banned Books Week that focuses on writers, publishers, and booksellers abroad who have been persecuted or jailed for their writing.

The focus of Banned Books Week is to educate the public about which books have been "challenged" in the last year. Challenged books have had formal complaints drawn against them by individuals or by political and religious organizations; these complaints most often request that the offending books be removed from the shelves of public and school libraries, or from classroom curricula. During the 1990s the American Library Association's Office of Intellectual Freedom registered more than 6,500 formal challenges, only 448 in 2001. The Office of Intellectual Freedom believes that less than a quarter of such challenges are actually reported to them. The hope of Banned Books Week is that, by disseminating this information, the challenges will remain only challenges, and the books will remain on the shelves.

As you might imagine, at least in the United States, the majority of these challenges are aimed at books for younger readers. The reasons vary, but fall into a few simple categories. Books are asked to be removed from the grasp of our children because of sexual material, obscene language, material unsuited to an age group, violence, homosexuality, occult matters, or the promotion of a religious belief contrary to that of the challenger.

The list of challenged books and writers changes every year, but there are some constants. Here are the top ten authors who were most challenged in the early years of the new century: J.K. Rowling, Robert Cormier, John Steinbeck, Judy Blume, Maya Angelou, Robie Harris, Gary Paulsen, Walter Dean Myers, Phyllis Reynolds Naylor, Bette Green. If you don't recognize some of these names, just ask your kids; most of these books are for teenage audiences, young adult novels.

It's not only books for younger readers that get challenged. Of the titles on the Radcliffe Publishing Course list of 100 top novels of the twentieth century, some 42 have received formal challenges, complete bans, or have been officially censored by a government agency.

While Banned Books Week may be primarily a symbolic act, it does have real impact. A customer comes into the shop, is drawn by the Banned Books Week display, and decides to finally read *Invisible Man* by Ralph Ellison. Encountering the book at home or on the train, the reader may be so moved by this work of the imagination that she might begin to question why someone, anyone, could possibly want to keep its light under a rock. And perhaps she will be the next citizen to stand up and say, no, you cannot legislate our imaginations.

A slow process, yes, but no less powerful.

|||||||

In the struggle against censorship and the fight to maintain the bookstore as a stronghold of free expression, the majority of work that a bookseller does to these ends happens on a day-to-day basis, on the floor. These battles are not formal or legal, and most often are entered into with customers and other members of the bookstore staff. A customer or a staff member might ask that a book be removed from the store's stock because it's offensive in some manner to someone. But while it's true that every bookstore carries some titles that will offend some people, the simple request to have it removed on such grounds can raise the most vehement refusals.

Every bookstore, by default, *doesn't* carry millions of different books. A bookseller may choose not to carry a book because it might not appeal to her customers, or because she just doesn't like the look of the cover. Of course, a bookseller can also carry books she knows will *not* sell. She might choose to stock every title by the Albanian novelist Ismail Kadare because she loves his work, even when she's pretty sure his name won't be popping up on any best-seller lists. There are countless reasons for a bookseller to carry or not carry a given title. But try to mandate what a bookseller may not carry, and there's bound to be resistance.

Any store that's carried *Playboy* or *Penthouse* magazines has undoubtedly received complaints; these magazines, it's often said, are degrading to women and detrimental to children, statements which are true enough. At Printers Inc. we did carry them, hidden behind the counter away from minors, but this precaution wasn't enough for one very earnest soul. This man complained about the magazines, and when showed where they were kept, was still not satisfied, so he began to circulate a petition in the local community asking that the store discontinue their sales. Decisions of this sort at Printers were arrived at by staff consensus during rather lengthy meetings. The arguments were vehement, on both sides. Yes, we all pretty much agreed, the magazines in question were not exactly pro-feminist, but what about the fashion magazines we carried—*Elle, Cosmopolitan, Vogue*—didn't these magazines also objectify women? Well, yes, but they were for women, not the men who would objectify them. How about *Playgirl*, then? Well, that did objectify men, but . . . And what about our books of nudes in the Art section? Pretty soon the list of what we would have to eliminate was growing rather long. The final consensus—do you know how hard it is to reach a consensus among thirty independent booksellers?—was that it was an individual's choice, and that it was our duty as a bookstore to carry what any of our customers might want. We also felt it was our duty to rebel against the force of censorship, even if in this case, it appeared only in the form of one earnest soul. The earnest soul continued his crusade for a few more days, only to discover that the good customers of Printers Inc. had more pressing matters to consider.

Another publication that has posed ongoing problems for booksellers is *The Anarchist's Cookbook*, a manual of subversive strategies for upending the status quo. There are truly dangerous sections of the book, especially the recipes for making bombs and weapons in your home. Other parts of the book are not lethal, however, and do represent a valid political point of view. A good many booksellers will not carry the book, most who do keep it away from minors, and still others treat it like any other book. It poses a thorny question, much in the same way that the choice to carry *Mein Kampf* is a difficult one for a bookseller. Should a bookseller stock a book that he finds objectionable, if only to uphold the free expression of a democratic society? Should the decision be left to the reader, the book's buyer? The answer to these questions for most booksellers is yes, absolutely. To deny access to such books is yet another erosion of a great, hard-won freedom.

The most intense battle over a single book at Printers Inc. was waged on behalf of Hugh Lofting's *Dr. Doolittle.* What could possibly be objectionable about the fantasy of a man who learns to talk with the animals? Published in 1922, the book uses a word that was all too common at the time, but one that's since come to be held as repugnant, the word "nigger." There is no defense for this word used in Lofting's context, no matter how lightly he employs it, and everyone in the store agreed with that. But did the appearance of the word in the book negate the book's entire value? Was the historical context enough to justify keeping the book? What about other books that used the word, but in a manner meant

to condemn racism rather than endorse it: *Huckleberry
Finn, Their Eyes Were Watching God*? Couldn't we trust
the parents who bought the book, or even the kids themselves, to know better? The argument went on for weeks;
meetings were held, letters posted, fierce discussions
took place in the stacks. Several compromises were pro-
posed. We might attach a note to each copy of the book
with a disclaimer, or we might go through each book
and remove the word, but these ideas felt too much like
a police action. In the end, we decided, as we had to, to
keep the book in stock. We could not change the past,
nor, it turned out, did we want to. To erase one part of
the past, we felt, was to threaten losing all of it.

When I was a sales rep I took part in a ferocious argument with a children's book buyer. The most embar-
rassing part of this scene, for both the buyer and myself,
was that it took place on the sales floor in the children's
section with dozens of customers listening in.

The book under discussion was a picture book, new
on the list, and I was showing it to the buyer to see how
many copies she'd like. It was a counting book, set in
the American Southwest, and the characters were rabbits dressed in the costumes of the region's Indian tribes.
I was going through my spiel, pointing out that the book
was thoroughly researched, and the costumes and activi-
ties depicted were authentic. The book buyer objected.
She would never buy this book for her store; she was
offended that Indians were being portrayed as animals
and felt that the book was dehumanizing. I countered

that many, if not most, children's books made animals out of humans. The argument escalated quickly, both of us refining and repeating our positions, a little more loudly with each repetition, until finally I lost my cool, rose to my feet, and found myself yelling in the middle of the children's section, "They're goddamn bunnies and it's a goddamn kid's book." After which I stormed out. Eventually this buyer and I became close friends, and later we would talk about how much we had enjoyed this argument, not for argument's sake, but for the passion therein, and the sense that a kid's book, one little book about rabbits, was important enough to lose one's dignity over.

||||||

Today there is a serious assault on the ability of bookstores and their customers to traffic freely in ideas and books. Section #215 of the Patriot Act, which was bullied into law after the events of September 11, 2001, gives the FBI the ability to obtain subpoenas and go through records of customer purchases. The FBI can do the same with libraries. After such searches, the FBI imposes a gag order on these booksellers and librarians, prohibiting them from discussing how many and which records have been seized. The customer whose records have been searched is never notified of these searches, nor is it incumbent upon the government to detail the searches publicly, nor to even admit to such searches. This portion of the Patriot Act was renewed in 2005 for an additional ten years.

Any time you use a credit card in a bookstore, or buy a book on-line or borrow a book from a library, the government can, without your knowledge, and at any time and without any stated cause, read over your shoulder. But trust us, the government says, we won't abuse this power. The Justice Department has so far refused to release any data on these searches and information seizures, including the simple figure of how many have taken place. In order to protect our freedom—according to the mandate of the War on Terror—our own government has declared our freedom violable; it has declared our privacy invalid while at the same time protecting its own right to secrecy.

The American Booksellers Foundation for Free Expression, the ACLU, and the American Library Association, along with other free-speech organizations, have filed lawsuits to counteract these extreme measures. Several bookstores have advised customers to pay in cash, so that their credit-card receipts will not reveal their reading habits to prying eyes.

Our government, sworn in by the power of the Constitution, feels free to overlook the first of the amendments guaranteed there, free expression of ideas. We are not told directly what to read or not read, but the books we purchase or borrow may be under government scrutiny. The battle against censorship, as old as books themselves, continues. What troubles me most about these reactionary developments, however, is that one of the broad targets in the ineptly named Patriot Act is the bookstore. For centuries, primarily from neglect, the bookstore has been the curious home of our most prized ideals. Now, it's under watch.

Days after the War on Terror was declared in the autumn of 2001, I dropped into San Francisco's City Lights, one of the world's great bookstores. Under the unimpeachable guidance of Lawrence Ferlinghetti— bookseller, publisher, poet—the store has published much great literature since it first opened in 1953, including the watershed publication of Allen Ginsberg's *Howl* (seized by customs officers on its second printing, but eventually liberated after a costly trial). On that day in 2001 when I visited City Lights, five enormous banners hung from the bookstore's façade and proclaimed the store's noblest and most powerful intentions. Each banner bore the image of a face gagged by an American flag, and this timely phrase, "Dissent Is Not Un-American."

The Yellow-Lighted Bookshop

I am promiscuous when it comes to bookstores. Every bookstore, from the most opulent Parisian emporium to the anonymous strip-mall shop in Tucson, offers its own surprises. Since the bookstore first beckoned me thirty years ago, I have been in thousands, as a customer, employee, sales rep, tourist. Each one has freely divulged its delights.

For the true lover of bookstores, there is no sense of right or wrong, cool or uncool. Although for many years I worked in independent bookstores and on their behalf as a sales rep and strongly believe they are an undervalued cultural institution, I cannot bring myself to draw a prohibition against chain stores. I live in an area that is piled to the rafters with world-class bookstores, which I visit on a regular basis and whose unread books clog my shelves, but I can't help from dropping into whatever airport shop I pass while changing planes in an anonymous city. I am fatally attracted to all bookstores.

Some Sunday afternoons, my daughter and I get it into our heads that we want to visit our local Borders. The store is enormous, with a café and a complete CD and DVD section, and it is always crowded. Knots of families, herds of students from the nearby state university and high schools, long lines. The children's section is spacious, with carpeted steps for lounging and reading together. There are some fish tanks, too, a nice touch. Maddy knows that she gets to choose one book to buy, I will choose a second for us, and I may even pick up something for her mother. And sure, why not buy something for myself? The store's loudspeaker buzzes with calls for more help at the register, the coffee bar hisses and steams. It may be that in this normally quiet neighborhood, on a Sunday that's long, languorous, and fogged in, Maddy and I have chosen to come here precisely for the hum and bustle of the place, to break out of our Sunday torpor and be around a lot of other folks. The store is both cozy and expansive, and it comes complete with hot chocolate and a cookie.

On a weekday evening, Maddy and I might stroll around the corner to Black Oak Books, a satellite of the much-respected Berkeley store. Black Oak is a Spartan shop, neat rows of blond shelves, little decoration, oddly pristine for a bookstore. There's a small selection of new books up front, but most of the shop is devoted to used books. The children's section here is small, part of its charm for Maddy because she can peruse all the offerings. We bid good evening to Carl and Maria who are chatting behind the front counter, then hunker down in the narrow aisle. We'll spend time reading two or three books through and finally pick one. What we love on this evening is that the shop is quiet, still, finite, and we seem to be the only customers. When we leave, the sky might be blazing evening orange and aqua in the west, and we know that bedtime, with one new book and two old favorites, is fast approaching.

I've been a West Coast boy my whole life and am woefully undereducated when it comes to stores on the East Coast or in the Midwest. My list of bookstores has been written, as I suppose are the lists we all carry, by chance and fortune and the odd turns of fate: I love the bookstores I do because I stumbled upon them. One of the pleasures of the bookstore is that there are so many and they are so varied. Let me proffer a brief selection of my favorite bookstores from around the world.

﹏﹏﹏

Close to Home: San Francisco

With Upstart Crow and Printers Inc. long gone, the bookstore where I feel most at home is The Booksmith in the heart of the Haight Ashbury district. For many years I have lived within walking distance of the store, and as a sales rep and a one-time Christmas-rush employee, I have come to know the owner and several members of the staff as friends. It's a narrow shop, crowded, and it sells more books than you'd think possible, the perfect urban bookstore. Along with its creative window displays, the store has a complete selection of titles, especially its thrilling and informative children's corner, a section built over seventeen years by the exemplary children's bookseller Joan Vigliotta. It is a bookstore that would enhance any neighborhood in any city.

But the three elements that make The Booksmith so seductive are less tangible than its selection of books. The person most often at the front counter or answering the phones is the store's owner, Gary Frank. Gary's never been content to sit in the back and order books, he's almost always there on the front lines, and it's this kind of involvement that makes an independent store thrive. Then there's the clientele and the street scene—old hippies, recycled punks, Banana Republicans, families of every blend, a smattering of tourists—that make the store a swell place to be alone among others.

Finally, but hidden from the public, is the store's employee restroom, which should be entered into the Retail Workers Hall of Fame. Covering the walls of the restroom are fifteen years of publishers' promotional materials that have been embellished by the store's employees, including ads for Good Dog Carl, Good Dog Carlos Santana, Good Dog Karl Marx, and God Dog Carl. My favorite bit, covered years ago by subsequent additions, was a poster for Joyce's *Ulysses* that reprinted the end of Molly Bloom's soliloquy, altered by a Booksmith employee to read, "yes, yes, oh yes . . . I will babysit for you Friday night."

City Lights Bookstore, justifiably famous for its publication of *Howl* and as a meeting place for the Beats, is still indispensable fifty years after it first opened. Near the corner of Columbus and Broadway, the store is surrounded by Chinatown to the west, old North Beach to the north, to the east a flank of strip clubs, and to the south the glittering skyline of downtown San Francisco. The location is abetted by the proximity of countless espresso joints, and three great bars, Vesuvio's next door and Spec's and Tosca across the street. On a bright San Francisco day, you can even spy Ferlinghetti himself standing on this corner, next to his bicycle, gazing up at this beautiful place he helped to create.

The location alone makes the trip worth the while, but once inside, the selection of books is overwhelming. Inside the front door, the register is crowded between a set of worn, narrow stairs, and a bounty of new titles is displayed in every crack and crevice. There's no other store in the world that so surprises me with its choices of featured books, from an Icelandic novel to a 500-page history of the shopping arcade. On the main floor, Fiction overflows, arranged in a manner unique to City Lights: American, English, European, Asian, Latin American, etc. There are also complete shelves of City Lights' own published titles, a massive selection of literary journals and magazines, and most intriguing of all, a rack of self-published poetry, many badly photocopied volumes with stapled bindings. The jewel of the store, however, is the poetry room, up the back stairs, a quiet haven of enormous possibilities, where the rush of the city dims and the quiet white space of the word overcomes.

City Lights is locally famous for its customer service, but of a type you might not expect. Nearby in North Beach is Caffe Sport, an old-style Italian restaurant where the waiters tell you what you may and may not eat, how much of each dish you are allowed, and basically harangue you throughout your meal. People wait in line for hours for this treatment. The customer service at City Lights is not rude, per se, it's, shall we say, preoccupied. Customer inquiries are often met with world-weary sighs, followed by mumbled directions and some vague pointing. If you're a regular at the store, after a while you no longer ask for help, but you can sit back and watch the tourists take a little ego bruising. I'm not complaining about the customer service, not at all; the store wouldn't be the same without it, and City Lights is just about perfect.

Another near perfect San Francisco bookstore is one that is literally incomprehensible to me. Kinokuniya Books in Japantown is big and busy, with periodicals, books, CDs, and stationery items. While the store has a small section of English titles on matters Asian, what most draws me here are the books in Japanese, a language I neither speak nor read, and where the front cover is on the back cover. Kinokuniya is a bookstore out of a dream, where the landscape is familiar, but the details baffling. It's no nightmare, though. It's here, where I cannot read the books, that the book as object, regardless of its content, holds its sway over me. I gaze at the foreign alphabet, pick up the slick paperbacks, wishing to crack the code, but finally am simply comforted to be surrounded by books.

||||||

Great and Small

If you want a big bookstore, you have to think cities, not books in cities, but whole cities of books, like novelist Larry McMurtry's Booked Up in Archer City, Texas (his hometown and the setting of *The Last Picture Show*), with four buildings of books laced into this small town (population 1,748). At Three Dog Books, also in Archer City, among other delights, you can purchase an alarming array of autographed McMurtry items, from first editions to original manuscripts. Alas, McMurtry recently announced that Booked Up will soon close, at least temporarily.

Perhaps the biggest bookstore of all is the village of Hay-on-Wye in Wales (population 1,500), with over forty antiquarian shops. Or Powell's City of Books in Portland, Oregon; Powell's is not an actual city, but carries enough books in a single location to qualify as one. Or the Strand in Manhattan, with "eight miles of books" (as the T-shirts have it) before you sleep. But all of these are stores that traffic primarily in used and antique books.

The shining example of the grand new bookstore is the Tattered Cover in Denver. When Joyce Meskis opened her store over twenty-five years ago, it was a cozy little place, but has proved so successful that it expanded several times in the first twelve years, until finally it moved, with the help of loyal customers, into a four-story location a few blocks from the original. The new location has an extensive newsstand, coffee bar, and full restaurant. A few years ago the Tattered Cover opened a second location, this one only three stories high, but with fireplaces, a children's tree house, and a reading hall. Together the stores carry over 150,000 titles, one million total books.

When you enter either of the Tattered Cover's locations, the size and selection have a calming effect, for you know you won't have to leave for a long time, and chances are good that if you're looking for a new book, you'll find it here. The size is reassuring rather than overwhelming. The stores are divided into small rooms and cutoff corners, which are appointed with comfy chairs, couches, and reading lamps.

But the book luster doesn't necessarily want an unlimited selection all the time, and if you're in the mood for something more intimate, there's the Grolier Poetry Book Shop, just off Harvard Square in Cambridge, under the sign of the three cats. The oldest all-poetry bookshop in the country, it opened in 1927 as a fine-press bookstore that featured poetry and avant-garde literature. When current owner Louisa Solano took over in 1979, the shop shifted its emphasis to trade publications and now stocks 15,000 titles of poetry, books on prosody, spoken-word recordings, and poetry journals. The interior is a simple square, whose ceilings seem taller than the shop is wide, a fitting size and shape for the thin books it houses. There's not much room here, but on a slushy Boston day, it's a fine place to elbow around the other customers in search of the next book.

In the southeast corner of Arizona, in the old copper mining town of Bisbee, you'll find Walter Swan's One Book Bookstore. When Mr. Swan self-published his first book, *Me 'n Henry,* the story of two young brothers in a bygone Arizona, he rented a small storefront in the downtown tourist district, where he still works most days. Next door you'll find The Other Book Bookstore, which Swan opened after writing a second book. The selection in The Other Book Bookstore is a little more varied these days and includes a cookbook by Swan and a collection of his stories for children. Despite the limited selection, you're welcome to stay as long as you'd like, maybe swap a few stories with the writer.

‖‖‖‖

The City as Bookstore

Booked Up in Texas and Hay-on-Wye in Wales can claim the title of book-cities, but there is only one city that can rightly call itself the City of Bookstores. Paris can, and does, claim any number of titles, but from the vantage point of one under the spell of book lust, Paris could easily be seen as an aggregation of bookstores that just happens to be connected by a historic river, crowded cafés, and splendorous architecture.

Paris offers everything. There are big chains, FNAC foremost among them, tiny used stores, and everything in between. But it's the range of international bookstores that most impresses me; there seems to be a shop for every language and culture—British, American, Australian, Hungarian, Greek, Italian, German, Russian, Polish, Portuguese, Spanish, Latin-American, Arabic, Indian, Japanese, Chinese, and at least two Canadian stores, one for books in English and one for books in Quebecois French. And those are only the ones I've discovered so far. Paris also has one of the most exhaustive collections of bookstores on the history of cinema, enough to occupy several days in tracking them down. And stores about cooking, architecture, decorative arts, anything and everything.

For the reader of English, there's no better place to start than Shakespeare and Co., on the Left Bank directly across from Notre Dame. This is not Sylvia Beach's shop, but one that pays homage to her store. George Whitman (who claims to be the illegitimate great-grandson of Walt Whitman) opened the current incarnation as Le Mistral in 1951 in an old grocery, a building first built in 1611, the same year Shakespeare wrote *The Tempest*. The shop immediately became a hangout for the expatriate literary community, and in the early sixties, Whitman changed the name to honor Beach's shop. Today, the front of the store is a mountain of new books, most made famous by their connection to Paris and Shakespeare and Co.—*Ulysses,* of course, books by Hemingway, Fitzgerald, Stein, even Kerouac. These are the same editions you could purchase at home, but they will always seem more romantic for having been purchased on the banks of the Seine.

After the touristy front room, the shop begins to resemble, if not in size at least in mood, the original Shakespeare and Co. On three floors, narrow corridors, stuffed with used books, lead to small bedrooms, also stuffed with used books and old couches and chairs. Tucked away in one of these corners, one can easily imagine the nearly blind Joyce trying to shush that bully Hemingway, so that he might get some decent reading in. It's as if the ghosts of the old shop moved here along with the name. If you hang out long enough, you're bound to be approached by one or another of a later generation's poets, who for a few francs, will offer to take you on a walking tour of literary Paris. Lots of ghosts here.

When I published my first novel, I gave a copy to my dear friend Ken Taylor, who was bound for Paris on his honeymoon, and asked him to sneak it into Shakespeare and Co. and put it on the shelf for me. A few years later, in Paris on my own honeymoon, I checked the shelves and found my novel missing; perhaps it was purchased by a traveler, or even better, stolen.

My first trip to Paris, before my honeymoon, was a great one—how could it not be—but I was suffering from a broken heart, and France was being pelted by hurricane-force winds. One rainy day, believing I could not get more homesick, I wandered a little west of Shakespeare and Co. and snuggled into the Village Voice, a cozy store with a rigorous selection of American and British literature. The store was meant to be a home-away-from-home, and on that day, and on subsequent, much happier visits, it's proved to be that. The store hosts readings by contemporary American writers, a reading certainly worth the trip for any writer even if she can't get the publisher to pay the airfare.

On that same broken-hearted trip I also discovered Galignani, the oldest English-language bookshop on the continent, founded in 1802, which today carries both French and English books. Hidden under the eaves of what was once the greatest arcade in Europe, it's a beautiful store, with warm, wooden shelves and tall, rolling ladders, and it still retains much of its 200-year-old flavor, an approximation of what the great eighteenth-century bookstores must have been like. On my first day there, again in the rain, but with rising spirits, I found it easy to imagine those English writers who passed through here at the beginning of their grand tours.

Paris, like any city—no, more than any city—constantly surprises me with its deceptions and discoveries. Go looking for one thing, and you're bound to find something even more spectacular. On my honeymoon, a month's splurge in stinky cheese, great wine, museums, and bookstores, Julie and I set out one morning to find a poster of Jacques Tati's film *Mon Oncle*. We were looking for a cinema bookstore we'd read about in Cadogan's *Paris*, but we never found the store, much less the street. However, we did stumble across the hippest little bookstore, Librarie 1789, under the ownership of Colette Loyer. Her selection was small but specific, mostly contemporary French writers, who were more experimental in nature, and an offering of literary and graphic journals I'd not seen elsewhere in Paris. After an hour in a store I had not been searching for, I left with the debut issue of a book review called *Calamar* (Squid) and a pocket-sized hardcover that was nothing but photographs of Samuel Beckett. It's been almost eight years since that trip to Paris, and I'm happy to report that Librarie 1789 is still in business.

To make the walk from bookstore to bookstore less book deprived, the good city of Paris has planted *bouquinistes* all along the banks of the Seine, those green wooden stalls that seem to have been there as long as the river itself.

⁗

It's a Bunny-Eat-Bunny World

Whether you have children or not, if you are under the spell of book lust, you must get to a store that specializes in children's literature. Many adults will find themselves in the children's section of their favorite store from time to time, but it's usually to purchase a gift for a friend or relative, or with one's own children. But there are many surprises that await the adult who ventures in out of purely selfish motives. Surrounded by copious illustrations of badgers, mice, dragons, wombats, kids who can fly, squids who can talk, and all the rest, we suddenly ask why we've made adult books so bland, so without color and other marks of distinction. It's not that children's books aren't serious, there's nothing unserious about them, but what is it about the interiors of most adult books that makes them too serious for illustration?

When I read an adult book, I'm often sure that will be my last reading of it. But children's picture books have a built-in repetition factor. Whether I'm reading the book for my own pleasure, or under my daughter's strict orders—"again, again"—I understand that I may be reading this book many times over the course of many years. An adult novel does take more time to read, but I'm not sure that's what keeps me from visiting it again. There are simply too many new books coming out that I want to read; I save my rereading for books I'm certain will offer up new pleasures. Rereading a favorite novel first read 5, 10, or 20 years ago, is a measure of our travel, how far we've come; it's a way of visiting an earlier self. Children's bookstores are perfectly suited for such sojourns. I do reread Faulkner, but I also reread Sendak.

Some of my favorite writers can be found in the Chapter Books shelves; these books, mostly novels, are for readers from seven through seventeen. Writers of these books have to paint an entire world and spin a compelling tale in under 150 pages, while still leaving the reader sated. There's been a lowering of the artificial barrier between Young Adult and Adult books in the last few years. Both kids and adults are fans of the Harry Potter series, Mark Haddon's *The Curious Incident of the Dog in the Night-Time,* and Philip Pullman's *His Dark Materials* trilogy, to name a few. Novels for younger readers have the same range of setting and intent as "real" novels, however. These writers who don't traffic in the overt fantasy that seems to sway adults to this section—Robert Cormier, Virginia Hamilton, Jerry Spinelli, Francesca Lia Block, Brock Cole, Louise Fitzhugh, et al—ought to be as read, discussed, and lauded as the most seriously considered adult novels. If you're embarrassed to shop in this section, just tell the clerk the book's for your niece.

A children's bookstore offers more than fiction, however. JoAnn King Jenkins, the children's book expert at Upstart Crow, once taught me that nonfiction books for children can be a great resource for adults. If you're interested in archaeology but know very little about it, it's not necessarily a good idea to try to read the definitive text by the world's leading expert, which could be daunting. A solid children's book on the subject can be a perfect place to start, for it usually takes care to spell out the bigger outlines of a subject and includes simple and explicated vocabulary, along with informative illustrations. From here, you can work your way up to more complex books on the subject with confidence. For example, visit *D'Aulaire's Book of Greek Myths* before moving on to Robert Graves. The children's versions of the tales are enchanting.

There are any number of children's specialty stores, all fighting the good fight, most of them not only selling books but actively involved in book fairs that materially benefit schools (and we know *they* need the money), and connecting authors and illustrators with their young fans. Hicklebee's in San Jose is an overstuffed store famous for its decor. There's a bunny-sized replica of the great green room from *Goodnight Moon,* cases of objects and characters from other books, and hundreds of illustrations and autographs (some of them on the walls and door jambs) by authors who've visited. It's a complete, tantalizing world. The next best thing to a trip to Hicklebee's with my daughter is a trip to Hicklebee's by myself.

The Red Balloon Bookshop in St. Paul, Minnesota, is a store much like Hicklebee's—with a staff overflowing with ideas and titles, and plenty of nooks for getting lost in. What they've done here, and what I've yet to see in other children's bookstores, is a coup of cross-marketing they should patent. Near the front of the store is a short but intriguing shelf of adult titles, new novels and nonfiction for mom and dad, so the whole family can leave happy. Or stay for as long as they wish. One-stop shopping.

||||||

In Transit

I used to have a favorite bookstore game when I had to fly somewhere. I always travel with three or four books in my luggage and one in my carry-on. Loaded down, I arrive at the airport with enough time to graze the airport bookstore. The game was, could I find anything at all I'd like to read? When I first started flying as an adult, airport bookstores weren't really bookstores, they were more like newsstands or drugstores—magazines, cigarettes, candy, cough syrup and aspirin, souvenir snow globes and ashtrays, a few cheap toys, and a wire rack or two of mass-market paperbacks. This was desperation reading, pages to stare at on a long flight, usually genre fare—romances, spy thrillers, science fiction. At the far end of the rack there was, invariably, a selection of "erotica" paperbacks with photographs of nearly nude models on their cheesy covers. A surprising number of these books concerned the exploits of oversexed stewardesses and airline pilots. Out of bookstore's mass-market selection, I would try to find something more literary. I'd usually see an Updike or two, maybe even a Vonnegut, and a few other authors who were literary but with popular appeal. The most interesting title I stumbled across in the airport bookstores of my long-agos was a collection of Coyote Trickster tales. I'm still not sure how that book got there, wedged between *Battle Station* and *Layover in Chicago.*

Today, thankfully, almost every large airport has an invigorating selection of hardcovers and trade paperbacks, classics and new titles, children's books, golf books, books about aviation history, regional travel and history guides, and business books. The erotica has been replaced by the short novels of Henry James.

Any form of travel—plane or car, train or ship—is an excuse to visit favorite bookstores and seek out new ones. At least once a year I go back east, and there revisit some favorite shops. When I go to South Hadley, Massachusetts, I have to stop by Odyssey Bookshop, if only for its great staff favorites and remainders, and while there, I'll take my purchases to the little coffee shop a few doors away, where they have a choice selection of used books. A trip to Asheville, North Carolina, isn't complete until I've been to Malaprop's downtown, where in their new location they've managed to keep something of the comfort of the previous one, though I do miss the sagging back porch. In Montpelier, Vermont, I recently visited a store I hadn't been in for twenty years, Bear Pond Books, which looks exactly the same as when I first visited, overfilled dark wood shelves, although the store has actually moved across the street. What first struck me about Bear Pond were the two signs hanging near the front entrance, each with an arrow pointing to a different half of the store; one sign said Facts, the other Truth, and I'll let you figure out which was for Fiction and which was for Home Repair.

Then there's the Double Hook in Montreal, Quebec, specializing in Canadian literature in English (Anglophone, and Francophone in English translation), which is a way of being in a foreign country, while still able to read the books. I never leave the Double Hook, or any of these stores, without a small stack. Again with the alas: Double Hook, I've just discovered, will be closing shortly.

It's not that I can't find the same books in San Francisco, I certainly could, if only by sitting in front of my computer. Nor is my impulse to buy books as travel souvenirs the literary equivalent of a T-shirt. I buy books when I travel because the bookstores I visit then surprise me with their selections. The new novel by Brazilian writer Moacyr Scliar may be in my local bookstore, or cheaper on Amazon.com, but I haven't stumbled across it yet. But if I'm at Square Books in Oxford, Mississippi, where a staff member has read the book or simply liked the cover, it might be displayed to catch my eye. Or it could be something as simple as the light in the Fiction section on that given day and how it strikes the book's colorful spine and calls out to me. Every bookstore has its own delights, and that's why we can never have too many. The hard part is getting all those books in the suitcase.

||||||

Odd Fellows

Let's consider those bookstores that can't help being something else. There are many bookstores-slash-cafés-or-restaurants, but there are other combinations that expand our notion of what a bookstore can be. Here's but a brief list.

Location can be everything. In the middle of the San Francisco Bay, with views of the city and the Golden Gate, the bookstore on Alcatraz Island helps to support this federal park and to educate visitors on the history of the island. Its best-selling books are memoirs by former prisoners, and guards and their families, which recount life during those years when the most dangerous criminals were shipped here to live out their sentences. The store's selection is limited, but the volume of sales is the highest of any nearby tourist attraction. Even if you don't actually buy a book, the view of the city, and the store's imposing stone walls, tell a great story.

Twenty miles south of San Francisco, in the coastside town of Half Moon Bay, is a combination bookstore derived solely from the owner's whim, Bay Book and Tobacco. Bay Book has a world-class science-fiction section, but there's also a walk-in humidor with a complete selection of cigars and pipe tobaccos. I've never figured out why this works in combination, but it does. Pipes and cigars are as slow to consume as books, and like books are both meditative and fiery. Even if you don't smoke a pipe, the close woodsy and cherry odors that fill the store can be transporting.

Farther north in California, in the redwood-forest town of Garberville, is a combination used bookstore and tattoo parlor. I had heard about it for a few years before I actually stopped in one day, and lo, there were rows and rows of books, and from the back of the store, a high-pitched whining sound that was unmistakable. When I approached the tattoo booths, I found a familiar face gently tracing the outline of a rose on a woman's shoulder; the tattooist and I had worked together at Printers in Palo Alto and this was her newest venture. We had a nice long talk, but I passed on the chance for my first tattoo. I can't remember the name of the store—Ink and Ink?

My favorite combination is the bookstore/record store. There are quite a few out there, but they tend to be decorous, with the volume kept low. I like it best when the record-store atmosphere infects the bookstore. Tower Records has installed book sections in most of its CD stores, but they also operate complete bookstores, most of which are adjacent to their CD stores. Tower Records is loud, very loud, and the stores are also visually complex, posters everywhere, color and light. Much of the CD-store ambience carries over into the bookstore; the shelves are jammed and messy, the back rooms are jungles of promotional materials and overstock, the music on the floor is loud and inappropriate (not a complaint), and the staff is decidedly rock-and-roll. It's a jumpy way to look for books, but sometimes, you just gotta jump. And besides, Tower Books, like their CD stores, is open 365 days a year, 9 a.m. to midnight.

‖‖‖‖

Out of Nowhere

I was fortunate to visit Prague in the winter of 1990, only months after the revolution. I had gone there for many reasons, not the least of which was to visit a city I'd come to know through the books of Kafka, Kundera, and Klima. I also had a somewhat quixotic and ill-conceived mission. I knew that the works of the best Czech writers had long been unavailable there, and the people of Prague, recently liberated from decades of censorship, were hungry for any books they could get their hands on. So I filled half a suitcase with English copies of Kafka and Kundera, which I placed, surreptitiously, on the shelves of the city's bookstores.

Late one afternoon on that same trip, I was directed, through a series of hand gestures, to a shop in a far corner of the old city, which turned out to be an art gallery that carried a selection of miniature books, each about the size of my palm. These books were hand bound in leather, with a unique tooled decoration on each cover. The breadth of titles was commendable, from Neruda to Tolstoy. I was struck by the notion that what the world needed was a miniature-book store (note the hyphen, a store for miniature books rather than a very tiny book-store, although that's not a bad idea either). It would be a small shop, of course, but the amount of titles would be vast, and you could buy almost anything there, from one of Keats's odes to a complete set of Proust's *In Search of Lost Time* (running to about 800 volumes in miniature).

Since then, I've tried to imagine bookstores that don't exist, yet should. If a miniature-book store, then certainly a folio-size store, where you could buy desk-size editions of any book you wished for a reasonable price. The Illustrated Store, which would have on offer lavishly illustrated editions of your favorites, new books and classics. Cookbooks, business books, too, and computer books. Make all books sensually alluring.

In his novel *If on a Winter's Night a Traveler*, Italo Calvino wrote a stirring description of the abundance of the bookstore:

Books You Haven't Read . . . the Books You Needn't Read, the Books Made For Purposes Other Than Reading, Books Read Even Before You Open Them Since They Belong To The Category Of Books Read Before Being Written . . . the Books That If You Had More Than One Life You Would Certainly Also Read But Unfortunately Your Days Are Numbered . . . the Books You Mean To Read But There Are Others You Must Read First,

the Books Too Expensive Now And You'll
Wait Till They're Remaindered, the Books ditto
When They Come Out In Paperback, Books
You Can Borrow From Somebody, Books That
Everybody's Read So It's As If You Had Read
Them, Too.

Calvino died in 1985 and left behind a list of the fifteen books he was planning to write. I would love to
open Calvino Books, preferably in Paris, where he spent
many years with his fellow Oulipo writers imagining
unimaginable books. At Calvino Books, you would find
a complete selection, in standard, miniature, folio, and
illustrated editions, of the books Calvino did not have a
chance to write. You would also find a section of your
favorite dead writers, and the books they were unable to
finish. There would be new arrivals every week.

In Paris there is today a bookstore with the wonderful title of Introuvable, literally The Unfindable. The last
bookstore I would imagine in my perfect bookstore city
would be the ultimate Introuvable, a bookstore that contained every book you'd been searching for—from the
one you had as a child about little purple ghoulies to
the tax guide that already had your information plugged
in. But you would only find the unfindable book if you
had exhausted all other possibilities. You would find the
unfindable only when you had given up hope.

New Arrivals

After 3,000 years of healthy expansion, during which time it adapted to and helped accelerate technological and cultural advances, the bookstore seemed to be in sudden decline during the 1990s. The larger bookstore chains expanded with vigor in these years, but independent stores seemed to be evaporating. Nearly two-thirds of American independents closed during a decade in which Internet commerce seemed nearly capable of destroying its brick-and-mortar competition. There have been other recent challenges to our sense of books and where we might buy them, notably the e-book, print-on-demand books, and mass-merchandisers. When we look at these misfortunes, especially the divisive argument of chains versus independents, I think it's important to remember the long history of the bookstore and its adaptability, the slow evolution of its form, and the quiet resistance it has shown to being replaced.

Is the bookstore dying? Will we all be forced to become computer geeks to get a glimpse of the new Stephen King? With nearly two billion books sold in 2004, trade publishing is perhaps healthier than ever.

The good news is that for the last five years book sales through independents have remained steady, about 15 percent of the total market share, and there is a sense that the mass closings of independents have leveled off and that the remaining independents are stronger than ever. The bad news is that the total bookstore market share, for independents and chains combined, continues to fall, from a 50 percent share in 1995 to around 35 percent in 2004. While the Internet accounts for about 10 percent of book sales today, increasing every year, the biggest loss of market share has been to mass-merchandisers, so-called big-box stores—price clubs, Costcos, Wal-Marts, etc.— especially in children's books. Subscription book clubs, gift outlets, and other venues are also increasing their volumes and eroding the bookstore's market share.

There's still a ton of books out there, we're just buy-ing them differently. The world, we know, has changed a good deal at the turn of this century, and there's not much point in lamenting what's been lost. However, it is provincial to focus only on what is rising, what is con-temporary and new; we should not forget what endures. The bookstore lays claim to our affections in ways that computers and warehouses have yet to replace.

IIIIII

Like many promises of the Internet revolution, the e-book seemed to have died a quick death when the dot-com bub-ble burst, along with all those other notions that sprang out of nowhere (did we really need a barbecue.com ?).

The e-book is a hand-held, battery-powered device that can download one or more books at a time, and that frees the reader from the hassle of turning all those pages. Like many DVDs, the e-book may also include supplemental material—criticism, cross-referenced indices, author biographies, visual aids, worksheets, etc. Among the promises of the e-book was that bookstores would no longer be necessary and that publishing could become a paper-free industry, eliminating overhead, labor, and freight. O brave new world. You'd go to your favorite web site, pay for and download your choice, then, one assumes, curl up in your favorite e-chair.

Publishers have spent a lot of money on the e-book, but readers have been resistant to the charms of this technology, unable to find an immediate advantage over the paper book. Much of this resistance is centered on the prospect of reading for pleasure from yet another computer screen. Early e-book screens were hard on the eyes and not very attractive. Companies have worked hard to develop screens that do not produce so much glare. Employing technology intended to bring Braille books to hand-helds, some companies have developed screens where the print rises up a bit, giving it a third dimension, a tactile and sensual aspect other computers have not yet replicated. See, there is a bona fide, constructive use for computer technology; it would actually benefit the world if visually impaired readers had unlimited and inexpensive access to books.

When the first Internet gold rush didn't pan out, some

e-book companies failed, and others cut way back. In the last year or two, the e-book industry has seen renewed investment and dedication. Currently there are over 50,000 e-books in print, a significant figure, but minuscule when compared to the number of hard-copy books in print. Consumer resistance is still strong, we may not be ready to curl up in that e-chair, but there is an other important place for the e-book in our literary culture. Technological and academic reference works, vital to many professionals, are often prohibitively expensive to publish, but an e-book version of these same works—medical manuals, comprehensive dictionaries, journals highlighting the most recent advances in any given field—can be produced far more cheaply and updated instantly.

For now, however, the flexible and durable technology of the printed book, as well as its quiet sensuality, are still what the general reader desires most. The simple test is this. Look around on the streetcar or bus or airplane and count how many e-books you see. None. We still prefer that quiet rustle of the pages, and besides, how do you press a wildflower into the pages of an e-book?

Another contender in the computers-will-run-the-universe competition is the print-on-demand (POD) book. With POD technology, a book is prepared for publication, but rather than printed in a run of 500 or 5,000 or 500,000 copies, the book merely waits for the customer to show up to be printed. The entire text of a book, including its cover, is stored in a computer and is accessed only when a copy is needed, thus printing the exact number of copies required. If only one customer orders a copy of a POD title, it can be printed in two minutes. The retail price of POD titles is somewhat higher than the traditional book, although they seem to be falling more into line as the technology improves. Like the e-book, this is a an advancement that can slash overhead, perfect for books needed in small quantities. It can also remove certain risks for the publisher; the 8,319 customers who want the book will buy it, and no remainders will ever make it to your local bookstore.

One problem with POD books is that, in order to keep the prices down, the discount offered to bookstores stands at around 20 percent, an untenable margin when most bookstores require at least a 40 percent discount on regular books. Another problem, one that is still being worked on, is that POD technology is primarily limited to paperbacks; hardcover and illustrated books are proving difficult to print cheaply and efficiently in this manner.

A vision that some POD advocates propose for the bookstore of the future is that it will be something like a photocopy shop. There'll be a front counter, a few computer terminals, but no stock of books through which to browse. Instead, you'll choose your book from a menu on a computer screen, order it with a point and a click, take your receipt, and wait for your number to be called. Kind of like ordering a combo meal at Carl's Jr. A horrifying vision for a book geek like me, but not impossible and not without its benefits. It's more likely that if POD technology finds a place in the market it will be included in the bookstore as a kiosk where you'll be able to order what you please. But what good is a bookstore that's uncluttered? What good is a bookstore if you can't browse?

|||||||

This is difficult for me to admit, but I have purchased books over (through, from, by, in cahoots with?) the Internet. New books, too. Not many, but enough to make me feel guilty. I can also admit, by way of expiation, that I have frequently used Amazon.com and other electronic bookstores as a source of information, first researching books on the Internet, then ordering them from a brick-and-mortar shop.

When Amazon.com and other electronic retailers first arrived, it did seem something of a miracle. Point and click, two days later your order is on your doorstep, brought to you courtesy of the post office, UPS, FedEx, whoever was cheapest or fastest. As the essayist Malcolm Gladwell pointed out in the *New Yorker*, the miracle of electronic commerce might owe more to a simple device for grading roads than to the invention of the pop-up window. This device was pulled behind wagons to make roads convex, the roadway higher in the middle, which allowed rain to drain off and keep the roads from becoming carriage-eating bogs. This simple machine arrived with, and because of, the advent of parcel post, a system that would connect the rural areas of the country more efficiently. Catalogue sales, through

Sears Roebuck, Montgomery Ward, and others, made it possible for the latest fashions and conveniences to find customers in the heartland. Talk about miracles: you could buy an entire house, as a kit, from Sears Roebuck, and assemble it on your property when it arrived via parcel post. A century later, in the 1980s, the growth in catalogue sales—L. L. Bean, Land's End, etc.—was promoted by the 800 number, electronic call centers, and the expansion of UPS. What made e-commerce possible had been set in motion over a century before. Stepping back a bit, we can see Internet commerce as nothing more than one giant catalogue.

The real problem with e-commerce, as with so many other Internet companies, was the business model it promoted. To win over customers, many e-tailers sold their products at ludicrous discounts, establishing a business model that did not require a profit. Amazon.com and other Internet book companies were leaders in this movement. The underlying theory behind this profitless model was, it seems, let's sell real cheap for now, get the customer hooked, and worry about the profits later. This is fine if you've got vaults of venture capital to play with and your main concern is the price of your stock's shares, but if you were a small bookstore attempting the same model, it's pretty certain that publishers would soon cut you off and the landlord would get a little testy. It's unfortunate that many bookstores suffered from competition with e-stores, competing against businesses with an insurmountable advantage.

The overall flaw in the Internet business model was that it rested on a premise that the Internet was so fascinating, quick, and efficient that consumers would shift all their time and attention to their computer screens, eschewing the world and its slownesses. The Internet bubble of the late 1990s burst in part, I believe, because we did find more important things to do than point and click. We still enjoyed, it turns out, going out into the sunshine, or the fog, or the rain. Computer screens alone did not make a life.

However, Amazon.com and other sites like it are not without benefit. If only because the growth of e-commerce hurt so many independent bookstores, the fate of the independent became newsworthy, and as a culture we began to value what we had taken for granted for so long.

Internet bookstores have indeed provided a valuable service to remote communities. A poet friend of mine lives on a small farm in rural Ohio, and she is a voracious reader. While it's not impossible for Pam to get to a good brick-and-mortar store, it is a long drive, and she can now order any book she needs from a number of web sites. It's also much easier for Pam, and the rest of us, to find and purchase books from smaller publishers who have typically had a hard time finding national distribution. Thanks to the Internet, every book now has national, even international distribution.

The Internet has also proved a boon to used bookstores. Through sites like abebooks.com, used booksellers from all over the world can display their inventories in a single marketplace. Used books aren't manufactured and cannot be ordered from the producer, and the ability to connect these stores and their unique stocks with far-flung customers has created an entire new marketplace.

But there are disadvantages to the electronic bookstore. It is possible at some sites to read a chapter of the book that interests you, but most often, all you get is a photograph of the book and comments from reviewers and readers. It's unlikely that a time will come when you can, for free, and at your leisure, read the entire thing. And it's even less likely that, while shopping in the virtual store, you'll be able to listen to the couple next to you talking about Paula Fox, a writer they just discovered, alerting you that not only has her first novel just been re-issued, but she's published a memoir, too. Yes, I can peruse a reader's review on a web site, but that's meant for me to see, not nearly as exciting as overhearing someone.

The Internet bookstore is here to stay, no denying that, and if the business models are adapted to the real world of commerce, then it will remain an important segment of the bookselling world. But the Internet bookstore places barriers between the reader and the book that leach much of the pleasure the brick-and-mortar store has always offered. Until the odor-replicator program is invented, how will we know if a book smells right? And if I want to sip on a latté while I'm looking at books, I might be forced to make it myself. At the Internet bookstore, I can choose from a bigger selection of titles than at Black Oak around the corner from me, but only one screen-page at a time. The Internet is too big for me to see the whole thing, too big for me to stumble on the next big surprise. The Internet is infinite; the bookstore is finite. Within this prescribed world, smaller and slower and inefficient, I can duck under the synergy of international global commerce, and discover, much to my surprise, the book I'd been looking for all along.

‖‖‖‖

I have a difficult time in mass-merchandise and warehouse stores. I tend to get short of breath, lose my shopping list and my concentration, and suddenly my cart is filled with fifty-gallon vats of hair gel because it seems too good a bargain to pass up. So, I don't normally go, but I have on occasion, and I could have purchased books at a steep discount, books I might even want to read. This is the arena of retailing that's cut out most of the bookstore market share recently, and like the Internet, it's undoubtedly here to stay. It's convenient, I understand, to pick up a couple of best sellers and some children's' books while you're out doing the shopping. The selection of titles in a price club or a Stuff'n'Things isn't very large, though, so it wouldn't seem to be in direct competition with the bookstore. But even though a price club doesn't sell a great number of titles, the few they do sell, they sell in enormous quantities, and this has made some publishers very happy.

The danger is that, as publishers come to rely on mass merchandisers for significant portions of their revenues, they pay more attention to the titles these outlets sell. If a book doesn't appeal to a price-club customer, it will not receive the same support as the newest spy-thriller-horror-romance-spiritual-guru-cookbook of the moment. In some cases, the book might not get published at all, if it has no Costco appeal. Nothing wrong with best sellers, mind you, unless profit-and-loss considerations narrow the variety of titles being published, which can harm the diversity of our culture, and make real bookstores less interesting places to be.

‖‖‖‖

The aggressive expansion of national bookstore chains in the 1990s, via the "superstore," probably did more to decrease the number of independents than any other factor. The discount policies of the chains were an important element to their success. By using their corporate size to obtain titles at discounts much higher than any independent could achieve, the chains were able to offer *New York Times* best sellers and other new and popular books at loss-leader discounts. The discounts were often so big that, during Christmas rush or a publicity spike, independent booksellers who were unable to find a title at a publisher or wholesaler, could go to a Barnes and Noble and buy a stack of five or ten at a deep enough discount that they could still turn a small profit on them by selling them at list price in their own stores.

While an independent's annual sales might not depend on best sellers, customers did disappear, not only going to the chains for one book at 40 percent off, but buying their full-price books there, too.

Deep discounts are not a new practice, and for over two decades groups of independent booksellers, sometimes with the help of the American Booksellers Association, have filed suits against certain publishers and chains, in which they claimed unfair trade advantages. None of these lawsuits have stopped discounting practices, but they have created tensions within the industry, pitting publishers against booksellers, and paying the mortgages of many a lawyer. To compete, many independent booksellers did, and still do, discount books, much more so than in the past, but it's a practice that does take money out of their already small profits.

The most aggressive facet of the chains' recent expansion was their scouting for new locations. Savvy, if not a little unseemly, chains often opened new stores in communities already served by vigorous independents. Using the size of their corporate assets to introduce and carry a store until it caught on, the chains were able to seduce customers with comprehensive and enormous stocks. In reconfiguring their images, the chains also took cues from the best independents, and introduced cafés, readings, newsletters, literary ambience, comfy couches, and other amenities.

I cannot, however, draw my line in the sand with chains on one side and independents on the other. To be honest, many of the bookstores that folded during the 1990s were small shops whose owners were simply unprepared for the vagaries of business competition. In my years as a sales rep, I often listened to the complaints of a bookseller whose shop was woefully understocked and understaffed, and who made no moves to compete. The life of a small-business owner is not an easy one, in bookstores or any other arena, but complaining has never been a solid business plan. When I survey the independents that are left today, they offer more services and variety than before, and can and do compete with the chains.

The chains are not evil corporate ogres (at least not yet). Chain bookstores, along with the changes they've made in their selections, making them more true to the bookstore spirit than to the department store's, have brought a greater selection of books to more people than the independents could have. Chain stores have made the book emporium a standard fixture in the great sprawl of American suburbia. A few years ago, while on vacation, I'd read that a new collection of short stories by the underappreciated writer David Huddle had just been published, and I found it in Boynton Beach, Florida. At a large chain store. Along with it, I found a selection of literary, popular, and other titles that would have been unthinkable in Boynton Beach twenty years earlier. I assert that this is a good thing for the bookstore, for the book, and for our culture.

This is where I eventually draw the line, not between

chains and independents, but between bookstores and the absence of them.

||||||

In Jason Epstein's *Book Business,* the renowned publisher and editor reminds us that for most of its history, publishing was a cottage industry. Since the 1970s, he writes, publishing has been transformed into a corporate culture, bigger publishers buying smaller ones, with larger media conglomerates buying these publishers and their new subsidiaries. Suddenly profits mattered. Many of the most important and successful publishers are now merely one piece of a media empire, and they must, like the film, television, radio, and newspaper divisions of these empires, make the bottom line work. Before this, Epstein relates from his vast experience, publishing was a small business, when even the most prestigious house might secure its future with one best seller, the profits from that book paying for other, less profitable titles. Corporate conglomeration, he adds, might have been a bit premature, for it's not clear that the book, the book of lasting value, the book not tied into a media synergy campaign, can survive the scrutiny of the shareholder's ledger.

Epstein's hope is that publishing will divide into two camps, one following the corporate path, the other returning to its more pedestrian roots. The new technologies do allow feisty individuals and smaller presses to create important publishing ventures without the sponsorship of large corporations. The upstart and innovative publisher Dave Eggers is an example of this possibility. Eggers had already been publishing his magazine *McSweeney's,* when his memoir, *A Heartbreaking Work of Staggering Genius,* became a huge best seller. Using this windfall, both in connections and finances, Eggers has turned *McSweeney's* into an exciting publishing house, one that does not rely on corporate shelter. One of his most audacious programs has been to publish his own first novel, *You Shall Know Our Velocity* (shades of the great English booksellers) through *McSweeney's,* and to make it available primarily through independent bookstores. Later he would sell the paperback rights to a corporate publisher, to keep the money coming in for his other projects. Eggers and others like him have chosen to focus on books that matter, trying to sell them to those readers who will care. He's not trying to take over the world, he's simply following his passions.

Like other developments in the book trade in the last thirty years, corporate ownership and accountability are not going to go away, but it's possible that the corporate structures have become so immense there's enough space for a cottage industry to establish itself in the cracks. Eccentricity always seems to find a way.

The future of our literary culture remains a heated issue, and the reports, if you believe them, are rather gloomy. The book is dead; the novel is dead; literacy is dead; the computer has triumphed. Despite these predictions, we're publishing more books than ever, and while there is a good deal being published that we probably won't be reading fifty, or even five years from now, this has always been the case. One look at the best-seller lists from the last 100 years will confirm this; most books fade away. But with so much being published, we're bound to find a few keepers.

It's important to remember that the death of literature, of a literate culture, is not an idea that we twenty-first centurions invented. In the nineteenth century, the invention of the bicycle was believed to mark the end of civilization; we would become leisure addicts and reading would surely cease. The same was said of radio in the 1920s, and of television in the 1950s. And at later dates, rock-and-roll, premarital sex, and the jet ski would be cited as literacy destroyers. Let's not forget that critics also wailed and gnashed their teeth when parchment replaced papyrus, and when Gutenberg printed his first Bible.

The literary culture within any society—those who cherish books, who read, write, publish, and sell them—has always been a small community. We must be realistic about the size of this community. The best-selling hardcover novel of 2004 was Dan Brown's *The Da Vinci Code,* which sold 4.3 million copies. In that year only eight hardcover novels sold more than one million copies. The average book has a print run of between 3,000 and 5,000 copies, and will never be reprinted. As I write this, in the first week of August of 2005, the dead heart of summer, the top-rated American television show was a rerun of *CSI: Crime Scene Investigation;* it had nearly 14 million viewers.

Literary culture may comprise only a fraction of our society, but its role is crucial. In the bookstore the individual can meet that culture, become part of a river of creation and imagination that has flowed without interruption for thousands of years. The bookstore is still the place where we may engage in the free and unrestricted congress of ideas. In the bookstore, we may be alone among others, but we are connected to others. Even if we were to stop all publishing today, it would take a very long time for all of our books to find homes, and we would still need the bookstore to offer its gathering place because the bookstore is not a virtual space, but a real one with many pleasures to offer.

At Black Oak Books around the corner from me, I have a nodding acquaintance with James, one of the employees. On my way into the store, I often catch him outside on a smoke break. We talk about the weather, the uprooted piece of sidewalk that's being replaced, the new Indian restaurant down the block. We also talk about books. We talk about new titles—have you read this? We are both fond of a freshly stacked feature table, and I have spent more than a few moments enjoying the bounty and order of all those books. We're both book geeks.

Today when I swing by, he's standing outside smoking, "It's kind of slow," he says. I'm on my way to pick up Maddy from school, but I have a few minutes to spare, a hunch that tingles the back of my neck, and I haven't been in the store for a few days. James tells me the new collection of Jim Harrison novellas has arrived, *The Summer He Didn't Die.* I've been reading Harrison for nearly thirty years, a writer I think should have parades thrown in his honor. Even though cash is tight these days, I know I'm going to buy it. I turn and go into the store.

Lewis Buzbee is the author of *After the Gold Rush* and *Fliegelman's Desire*. He lives in San Francisco with his wife and daughter, and is almost always in a bookstore.

The Yellow-Lighted Bookshop has been typeset in Concorde, a font designed by Günter Gerhard Lange in 1967. Book design by Wendy Holdman. Composition at Prism Publishing Center. Manufactured by Maple Vail Book Manufacturing on acid-free paper.